DOS 6

Quick&Easy

A Visual Approach for the Beginner

Welcome to **Quick & Easy**. Designed for the true novice, this new series covers basic tasks in a simple, learn-by-doing fashion. If that sounds like old news to you, take a closer look.

Quick & Easy books are a bit like picture books. They're for people who would rather see and do than read and ponder. The books are colorful. They're full of illustrations, and accompanying text that is straightforward, concise, and easy to read.

But don't waste your time reading about our **Quick & Easy** books; start learning your new software package instead. This **Quick & Easy** book is just the place to start.

DOS® 6
Quick&Easy

Ron Mansfield

SYBEX®
San Francisco • Paris • Düsseldorf • Soest

Acquisitions Editor: Dianne King
Developmental Editor: Sharon Crawford
Editor: Richard Mills
Technical Editor: Lonnie Moseley
Book Designer: Helen Bruno
Production Artist: Claudia Smelser
Technical Art and Screen Graphics: Cuong Le
Desktop Publishing Specialist: Suzanne Albertson
Proofreader/Production Assistant: Stephen Kullmann
Indexer: Ted Laux
Cover Designer: Archer Design
Cover Illustrator: Richard Miller
Screen reproductions produced with Collage Plus.

Library of Congress Card Number: 93-84948
ISBN: 0-7821-1120-3

Manufactured in the United States of America
10 9 8 7 6 5 4 3 2 1

To my young son, Adam, who reminds me that computers—like life— should be fun.

ACKNOWLEDGMENTS

●

Only big families write books. It all starts with wonderful folks like Rudolph Langer and Dianne King and Kenyon Brown, who help match writers with projects.

Then there's Richard Mills, the guy who got stuck wrestling with my misplaced commas, embarrassing lapses in grammar, and the overall content of the book.

In another part of the world, Lonnie Moseley made sure things were technically correct, and repeatable.

Production is never easy, particularly on the tight deadlines computer-book publishers are required to meet these days. Throw in a hundred or so color screen shots that need to be placed at just the right spots in the text, and it's a miracle that you are holding this book in your hands at all. If it weren't for the tireless work of Suzanne Albertson, Stephen Kullmann, Cuong Le, and Claudia Smelser, you'd be reading someone else's book now.

So many other people helped that it is impossible to mention them all—the sales and marketing departments, the printers, warehouse people, your local bookseller—you get the picture.

Thank you sincerely, one and all!

Contents
at a Glance
●

Contents

INTRODUCTION

●

Chances are, you're reading this book because you don't want to become a computer expert. You need a PC for work or play, and you don't care a whit about DEVICEHIGH or NOEMS or HENWAYS. I not only understand, I'm envious. There are tens of thousands of things I wish I didn't know about my computers. And I've left most of that stuff out of this book. The truth is, the majority of DOS trivia is useful only if you are a programmer or consultant, or computer addict. And you're not one of *those,* are you?

Here, you will learn how to use DOS to run contemporary programs (like WordPerfect and Lotus 1-2-3 or Excel). You'll learn how DOS can enable you to organize and quickly find the information stored on your computer.

If you've used earlier versions of DOS, this book will show you what's new in DOS 6. Plus you'll learn some tricks you'll wish you'd discovered years ago.

There are the inevitable step-by-step exercises—recipes for everyday DOS tasks, if you will—but I've preceded them with just enough background information so that you will understand what's going on. The large number of full-color illustrations in the book will help you to follow along at your computer.

And here's the best part: I'll even tell you when I think you should *not* use DOS directly—when to use embellishments like a mouse, the DOS Shell, or Windows. Bill Gates won't mind. He's already sold you most of these new toys—or will eventually.

Along the way you'll discover that DOS 6 is really quite patient. It's capable of offering instant online help when you forget what to type or when you get into trouble. Speaking of which, we'll touch on viruses, disk failures, and other nightmares. The emphasis will be on prevention, but you'll also learn what to do, what *not* to do, and when to get knowledgeable assistance.

> **• Note** If you are using an earlier version of DOS (version 5, for instance), most of the lessons in this book will still work, but you may want to upgrade to MS-DOS version 6 to take advantage of the new version's improvements.

How This Book Is Organized

This book has 20 "lessons" organized in a way that makes sense to most of the DOS users I've taught. This is one of those books that you can devour in an afternoon or savor for weeks, a nibble at a time. We'll start with some background information in Lessons 1 and 2—then, perhaps ten minutes from now, you'll see how to run programs in Lesson 3. Truthfully, you may be able to stop at the end of the third lesson until your hard disk gets full of old files, or until you misplace three days' work and need to find it. But if you have the time, don't quit reading so soon. Keep at it.

The pace quickens, and things start to make more sense. You'll learn to organize and view the contents of your hard disk; name, rename and move files; recover files you've accidentally deleted; and get online help. You'll develop a backup strategy so that your important computer-based records won't be irretrievably lost because of a disaster, burglary, or hardware failure.

By the time you hit Lesson 13, you'll no longer feel inclined to walk away when the talk turns to computers at cocktail parties. Lessons 13 through 20 help you hone your skills and contain tricks of interest to anyone who spends a lot of time computing. If, on the other hand, you are one of those people who just uses Windows, WordPerfect, and another program or two, and never inserts floppies in your computer, you may be able to skip Part Three altogether.

WHAT YOU NEED TO GET STARTED

Because We Said So, That's Why

It figures. You bought this book because I promised that DOS could be quick and easy. Already I'm starting with the rules and conventions and cautions. Sorry, pilgrim, this little side trip is unavoidable.

Spaces and Periods Matter!

If DOS expects you to type one space and you type two, or if you don't type any spaces, things may not work properly. Touch typists often add extra spaces or unnecessary periods when working with DOS. Stop that!

Following Keypress Instructions

Occasionally, you'll be asked to press two or more keys *simultaneously*. This is indicated by hyphens. For example, Ctrl-C means hold down the Ctrl key while you press the C letter key.

When you are expected to press and release multiple keys, one at a time in a sequence, this book will show the keystrokes separated by a space. For example, when you read "press Alt-F X", here's what to do: Hold down the Alt key, press and release the F key, then press and release the X key.

What You Need to Get Started

To keep this from becoming the *Not So Quick & Easy* book, I'll assume that your computer is set up, that DOS 6 is properly installed, and that someone has shown you the computer's power switch or switches. By the time you get to Lesson 13, you might want to have some floppy disks to play with and a caffeinated drink. If you plan to use the DOS Shell tricks described in most lessons, your computer will need a properly installed mouse, trackball, or other pointing device, which will make things quicker and easier.

Except for a sense of humor, that should do it. Let's cut to the chase. After all, DOS 6 isn't a lifestyle, it's just a tool.

Getting Started

What's DOS and why do you need to understand it, anyway? How can DOS help make your life easier? How do you use it to run programs? You'll learn these things and more in Part One.

What's DOS and Why Do You Need to Understand It?

MS-DOS, or PC-DOS, or Compaq DOS, or DOS by any other name can help you

- Run programs like WordPerfect, Flight Simulator, and Windows

- Organize the contents of your disks

- Get rid of old stuff when you're done with it

- Exchange floppy disks with other computer users

- Protect your computer-based information

Computer freaks and professionals use DOS to do other things, like fine-tune the performance of computer systems or change the number of characters displayed on-screen. You've probably got better things to do.

How Much Do You Need to Know about DOS?

If your computer is equipped with Microsoft Windows, and if all the programs that you use are true "Windows" versions, most days you'll need to know next to nothing about DOS! You will routinely use DOS to run

Windows, and then employ Windows itself to do nearly everything else. Windows and DOS work together with very little human intervention. In fact, you can set up DOS so that each time you power up your computer, DOS will run Windows automatically.

But life's rarely that simple. Many older programs can't be run directly from Windows; others run under Windows, but SLOWLY. Things that are very easy to do in Windows with a mouse are very difficult to do in Windows sans mouse. If your mouse dies, or if you leave it home, or if you ever sit down at a "non-Windows" computer, you'll be glad to know how to deal directly with DOS. So, whether or not you are a Windows user, keep reading.

What Is DOS, Anyway?

DOS is an acronym for disk operating system. MS stands for Microsoft. MS-DOS—well, you get the picture. DOS is actually a collection of programs (instructions) that your computer uses to control things like your keyboard, disk drive, and display. DOS does most of its everyday tasks automatically, beginning with when you turn on your computer. From time to time you'll want to tell DOS what to do and where to go. You do this by typing instructions or pointing and clicking with a mouse.

The DOS Command Prompt: Waiting for Your Instructions

If you haven't already done so, turn on your computer and its display now. Shortly after you flick on your hardware, you'll see a blur of babble, ending with a few cryptic characters on a line of their own. It will look something like what you see on the top of the page.

Near the bottom of your screen you should see a disk-drive letter (usually C), a colon (:), a greater-than symbol (>), and ofttimes, other text between the colon and the greater-than sign (C:\> or C:\DOS>, for example). This ragtag line of characters is reverently referred to as the

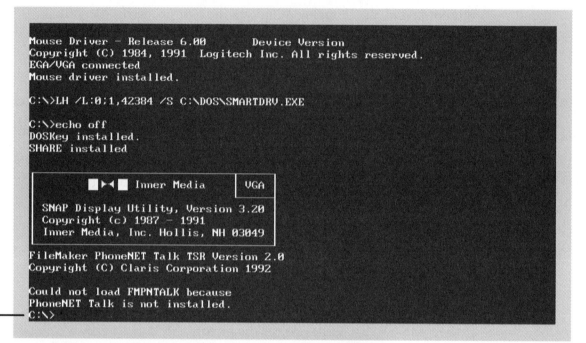

```
Mouse Driver - Release 6.00       Device Version
Copyright (C) 1984, 1991  Logitech Inc. All rights reserved.
EGA/VGA connected
Mouse driver installed.

C:\>LH /L:0;1,42384 /S C:\DOS\SMARTDRV.EXE

C:\>echo off
DOSKey installed.
SHARE installed

     ■►◄■ Inner Media      VGA

SNAP Display Utility, Version 3.20
Copyright (c) 1987 - 1991
Inner Media, Inc. Hollis, NH 03049

FileMaker PhoneNET Talk TSR Version 2.0
Copyright (C) Claris Corporation 1992

Could not load FMPNTALK because
PhoneNET Talk is not installed.
C:\>
```

**There are actually several DOS prompts in this illustration.
The last one is all that counts—for now.**

DOS command prompt, but everyone I know calls it the "DOS
prompt" or simply "the prompt." See if you can spot the prompt in the
preceding illustration, then locate the DOS prompt on *your* screen.

What's All This Other Nonsense?

Above the DOS prompt on your screen, you'll probably see copyright
notices, disk cache statistics, error messages, shoe sizes, earlier DOS
prompts, and lord knows what all. Chances are you can ignore everything above the last prompt. All that stuff is there to help techies troubleshoot. As long as you see a DOS prompt (C:> or perhaps C:\> or
something like it), you're OK and can skip ahead to the section "Typing a DOS Command."

What If I Don't See a DOS Prompt?

If you don't see the prompt but see a "menu" containing a list of numbered choices, like "WordPerfect" or "Accounting" or whatnot, or if you see a Microsoft Windows window, someone has probably made life "easier" for you by isolating you from DOS.

If you are staring at a list of program choices and are lucky, there's a DOS prompt at the bottom of the list. Or perhaps there is a choice on the menu like "DOS" or "Exit." Try them. See if you can reach the DOS prompt this way.

If you are in Windows, exit Windows before continuing with this lesson by pressing **Alt-F X ⏎**. You should see the DOS prompt after you exit.

> **● Note** To follow the keypress instructions above, hold down the Alt key and press F. Then release both keys, press X, then press ⏎, called the Enter or Return key.

If all else fails, consult the documentation that came with your computer, or ask a guru before you continue. Sorry. Nothing's really quick and easy anymore.

How Come My Prompt Looks Different from the Examples?

In Lesson 15 you'll learn how to personalize the appearance of the DOS prompt (to make it easier to tell "where you are," for instance). But at the moment, it's enough to know that your prompt may look a little different from those in the examples, and that's OK.

Typing a DOS Command

You tell DOS what you want to do by typing instructions called *commands*. There are over a hundred commands and many variations of each. You'll probably need to learn only a dozen or so.

Just for the heck of it, try the DOS directory command now. In case your momma never told you, the command is DIR. Here's how you do it.

With the little flashing bar (called the *cursor*) sitting to the right of the DOS prompt:

1. Type dir (no need to capitalize here, but it's OK if you do).

2. Press ↵. Information should scroll onto your screen.

The DIR command lists file information. Try it now just for kicks.

```
C:\>dir

 Volume in drive C is VOLUME 1
 Volume Serial Number is 1A57-78F1
 Directory of C:\

COMMAND  COM     52925 02-12-93   6:00a
TIF             <DIR>       03-09-93   6:29p
BAT             <DIR>       03-09-93   6:30p
WINA20   386      9349 02-12-93   6:00a
DOS             <DIR>       01-08-92  10:35a
ADAM            <DIR>       03-09-93   6:36p
UTIL            <DIR>       01-08-92  10:36a
WINDOWS         <DIR>       01-08-92  10:36a
WINAPPS         <DIR>       01-08-92  10:38a
DOSAPS          <DIR>       03-10-93   9:25a
TEMP            <DIR>       03-10-93  10:03a
PNTALK          <DIR>       03-18-92   4:43p
CONFIG   SYS       327 02-23-93   3:07p
AUTOEXEC BAT       681 03-10-93   9:52a
SNAP            <DIR>       02-25-93  11:49a
        15 file(s)      63282 bytes
                     42483712 bytes free

C:\>
```

Whoa! An alphanumeric explosion. Actually, it's just information about some of the files on your computer's hard disk. You've successfully executed the *directory* command, which you'll learn all about in Lesson 4. If, instead of a file list, you see the phrase "Bad command or file name" on your screen, check your typing and try again.

Once you've seen a directory list, try using CLS, a DOS command that clears the screen:

1. Type **cls** (again, no need to capitalize).

2. Finish the command entry by pressing ↵.

Your screen should clear and redisplay the DOS prompt:

Ahh. Better. That's the essence of telling DOS what to do. Type a legitimate DOS command at the prompt and press the **Enter** key. As you will see later, you can even issue DOS commands while using other programs, like the DOS Shell.

Switches and Other Command Modifiers

Sometimes you can change the behavior of a DOS command by typing something extra after the command itself. For instance, you can often type things called *switches*. Switches consist of a slash (/) and one or more letters. To see a really dramatic example, let's use the DIR command with its "S" switch. Try this:

1. Type **dir/s** (no need for a space between the command and the switch).

2. Press ↵.

The names of all of your files—a seemingly nonstop mess—should begin to scroll past. Don't worry, this will stop eventually.

In effect, you've used a switch to tell the DIR command that you want to see a list of *all* files on the disk. You'll learn a lot more about switches later, including some that will make DOS pause long enough for you to read lists like the one that just flew past.

The DOS Shell: An Easier Way to Work

The DOS command line has been around for years. It's a pretty unintuitive way to work. You need to remember a lot of obscure keystrokes and don't really see much of what is going on. Microsoft has provided several tools to make working in DOS easier. One of those tools is the *Shell,* more properly called the *MS-DOS Shell.*

What's the DOS Shell?

The Shell is a "visual alternative" to the DOS prompt. It's a program that makes it easy to see how your computer's files are organized. And it lets you issue DOS commands by pointing at things with a mouse or picking choices from drop-down menus. It even offers built-in, online help.

Starting the Shell

To start the Shell, type

DOSSHELL

at the DOS prompt, and press ↵. Notice the spelling: *not* DOSHELL, or DOS SHELL, or even DOSS HELL (my favorite), but DOSSHELL.

```
C:\>dosshell

Microsoft (R) DOS Version 6 MS-DOS Shell
Copyright (c) Microsoft Corp 1993. All rights reserved.
```

If all goes well you'll see some version and copyright info, followed by a screen like this:

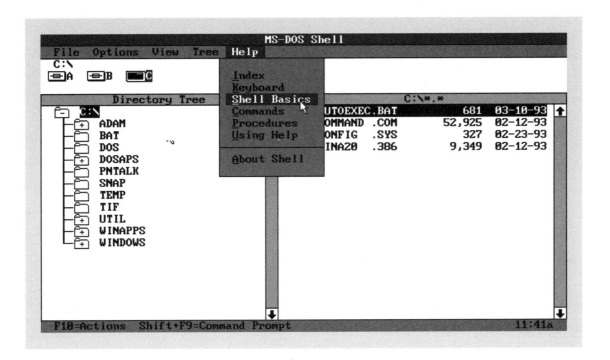

If you see an area called "Main" at the bottom of your screen, just select Single File List from the View menu to see the same view as shown here.

● Note Throughout this book, you'll see how the Shell can make things quicker and easier. While it doesn't bring "Macintosh simplicity" to your PC, the Shell's a big help, and worth learning. Don't skip over Shell information too quickly, particularly if you are not a Windows user.

Now, let's turn to an important topic that the Shell can help you understand—how disks are organized. That's the subject of Lesson 2.

2

How DOS Helps You Organize Your Files

Computer information is stored in *files* on *disks.* For our purposes, there are two general kinds of files: *program files* and *data files.* Program files (also called *executable* files, or simply *programs*) teach your computer how to do various tasks like word processing, game playing, and bookkeeping. Data files contain *information* used by programs—like lists of names for junk-mailing projects, checking-account information for your bookkeeping program, and so on.

Today's computer disks often contain thousands, or even tens of thousands, of files. The sheer number of files on a disk can be overwhelming. For this reason, file collections are usually grouped together, or "organized," in much the same way you might organize the paper files around your office. Computer files are placed in *volumes, directories,* and *subdirectories,* which some people like to think of as the electronic equivalent of filing cabinets and file folders. Let's take a closer look.

Disk Drives

Your computer probably has multiple disk drives—at least one of them a floppy drive, and another, called a hard drive—normally hidden under the covers of your computer. (Never mind that floppy disks are not usually very floppy these days and that hard disks are not all that hard—that's what they're called.)

If you work in an office, your computer may also be connected to a *network* that lets you access information on other disk drives in other machines within the office or even across the world.

In any case, you'll surely have at least two disk drives. Sometimes, DOS needs to know which drive you intend to work with, so each is identified by a letter and a colon.

Typically, floppy drives are called A: and B: drives. (If you have only one floppy drive, it can be used as both the A: and B: drive, for purposes that will become apparent later.)

If you have only a single hard disk, it is usually called the C: drive. If you have more than one hard disk, are connected to a network, work for NASA, or have an otherwise confusing life, you may also have drive names like D: or AZ:.

Directories: Manageable Collections of Files

The contents of a disk (be it floppy or hard) can be broken down into smaller units called *directories* and *subdirectories*. For instance, if you do a lot of work for the PTA, you might want to organize your PTA-related computer files into subdirectories. Perhaps you'll decide to keep word processing documents detailing PTA meeting agendas in one directory, database files containing PTA membership information in another, PTA newsletter desktop-publishing projects in another, and so on. You can further subdivide things by creating subdirectories within subdirectories. You could have different subdirectories for each *year's* newsletters, for instance.

Look at the *directory tree* on the left side of the screen in the following example. It shows you how the volume (the disk) is organized. In this example, a floppy disk (drive B:) has a subdirectory called PTA. Within the PTA subdirectory, you'll see other subdirectories (AGENDAS, MEMBERS, etc.) The NEWSLTRS subdirectory has two subdirectories within it—92 and 93. The right side of the screen shows the names of the files in the 93 subdirectory (FEB_NEWS.DOC and JAN_NEWS.DOC), because the 93 directory is higlighted in the directory tree.

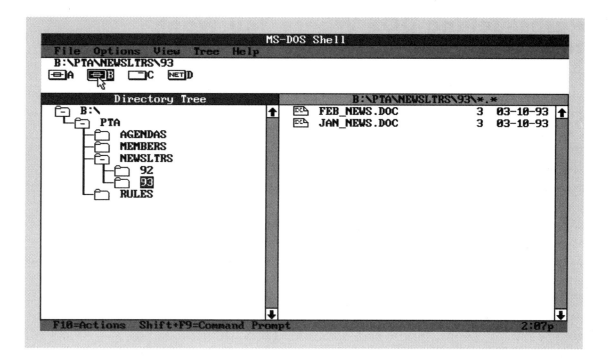

> **• Note** As you can see, it's possible to have subdirectories within subdirectories within subdirectories and so on, but more than three levels of this is usually overkill and often more trouble than it's worth.

The Root Directory: Mother of All Directories

Each volume starts out with something called the *root directory.* This is the "topmost" directory. Back in the earlier illustration, the root directory is called B:\.

All subdirectories are kept within the root. The name of the root directory is always \ (a backslash). Thus, the root directory for drive C is C:\; for drive A, the root is A:\; and so on. Some computer folk call the root the *parent* directory and subdirectories the *children.* Just thought you'd like to know.

Paths: Telling DOS Where You Want to Work

Frequently, when you tell DOS to do something, you'll need to be specific about where files are located and where you want things to happen. For instance, if you've stored the JAN_93 newsletter file in the 93 subdirectory within the NEWSLTR subdirectory within the PTA subdirectory on drive B:, DOS needs to know that before it can work with the newsletter file. You tell DOS where to look by specifying the *path* to the desired file. There are many different ways to do this.

When using Windows or the DOS Shell, you can often simply point to the file of interest, click the mouse button, and your computer will take it from there. In effect, the computer figures out the path by watching where you point.

When dealing with the ugly old DOS prompt, however, you may need to type the "directions," or the *path name,* that DOS will use to locate the desired file. (Whether you point or type, you are telling DOS the path name for the file.) In the newsletter example, the path name is

        B:\PTA\NEWSLTRS\93\JAN_NEWS.DOC

Phew! I'd rather point than type that, wouldn't you?

At any rate, that's what a path is: a list, including a drive directory and subdirectory names, telling DOS where to find something or where to do something. Notice the backslashes separating each subdirectory in the path. Keep reading. This will all make sense soon if it doesn't already. And a properly set-up computer will take care of a lot of the path-name details for you.

What's the "Current," or "Active," Directory?

Knowing what a pain in the rump it is to type all that path stuff, DOS lets you switch to a particular subdirectory and stay there until you are ready to move on. This directory becomes the *current directory,* also referred to as the *active directory.*

Switching to a particular subdirectory can sometimes save you time and effort, as you will see soon. And sometimes your computer will change directories for you without even asking your permission. In these cases, it is often important to know the name of the current directory so that you can figure out where you are. DOS can tell you the name of the current directory in a number of ways, as you will see.

How Are *Your* Files Organized?

It's time to try some experiments, so fire up your PC, if it's not already on, and run the DOS Shell if it is not yet visible (type **DOSSHELL** and press ↵ at the DOS prompt, remember?).

The first thing the Shell does is examine your hard disk to see all the subdirectories you have. After this (it can take a moment or two), you'll see a display similar to the example on the next page, except it will show the subdirectories and files contained on your hard disk. Hopefully, you'll see the directory tree on the left side of your screen. The right side of the screen should list the files contained in your root directory.

The area directly above the directory tree should contain little pictures of two or more disk drives (these pictures are called *icons*). There's a letter next to each disk icon denoting the drive letter (A, B, C, and so on).

One of the icons and its letter are highlighted—the C drive in the illustration. This is the DOS Shell's way of pointing out the *active,* or *current,* drive.

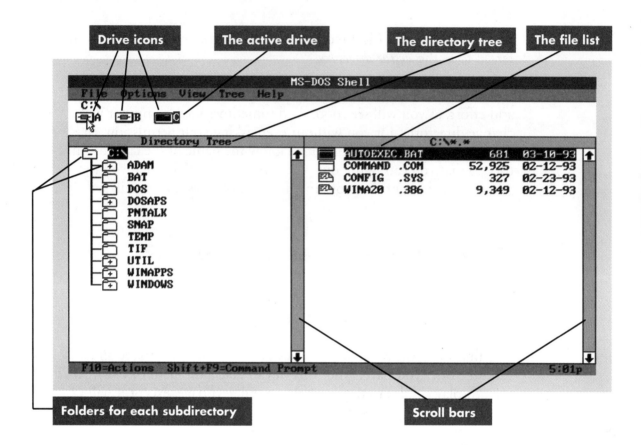

Drive icons

The active drive

The directory tree

The file list

Folders for each subdirectory

Scroll bars

The little folder icons in the directory tree represent subdirectories. A plus in a folder tells you that a subdirectory has its own, additional subdirectories.

If you have a mouse, take a moment now to point to any folder on your screen that contains a plus (+) and click (press the left mouse button). You should see additional folders as you reveal the next "level" of your disk's organization. Later in this book you'll learn how to reorganize things. For now, just be sure you understand that disks can have multiple subdirectories, including subdirectories within subdirectories.

Incidentally, if you don't have a mouse, you can still look at subdirectories in the DOS Shell, but it's more work and possibly a tad confusing. You'll learn how in Lesson 4.

Switching Drives

Normally, when you start any contemporary DOS-based computer, drive C: becomes the active drive. It's easy to switch to a different drive—to work with floppies or over a network, for instance.

When in the Shell, you can simply point to icons of disk drives and click with a mouse button to switch drives. When you change to a floppy drive in the Shell, make sure you have a disk in the drive first, or be prepared for the wrath of DOS:

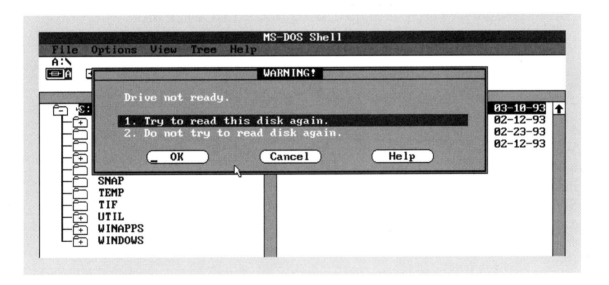

Nothing confounds DOS more than an empty disk drive, particularly if you are working with the dumb old DOS prompt.

Incidentally, at the DOS prompt itself, you can type a drive name (B:, for instance) to switch drives. You'll get step-by-step instructions for all these tricks in later lessons.

● **Note** When putting a disk in a floppy drive, put it in label side up, and be sure the disk drive is empty. You can easily damage a floppy drive by trying to force two disks down its throat. By the way, preschoolers seem compelled to put things in floppy slots—Post-it notes, knives, self-portraits in crayon, you name it. Try to minimize this.

Usually, in multidrive machines, floppy drives are physically stacked one on top of the other. The top drive is normally A: and the one beneath (if there is one) is B:. All bets are off if your computer is on its side. Ask the guru, or experiment to discover what's what. Mark them A: and B: if you are forgetful.

About File Names and Extensions like .EXE and .TXT

We're almost ready to run some programs, but several other things are worth mentioning. When using the Shell to look at your files, did you notice that none of the file names was more than eight characters long? Well, that's no coincidence, it's the law! MS-DOS file names must not exceed eight characters (dumb). Names cannot contain *spaces* (dumber still), or any of the following characters:

    * ? / \ | . , ; : + = [ ] { } & ^ < >

Geeze.

On the brighter side, you can add things called *file extensions* to file names. They always start with a *period* (that figures, huh?) and can be up to three characters long. Examples of file names with extensions you might have seen include AUTOEXEC.BAT, COMMAND.COM, and README.TXT.

Many extensions are used by DOS and other programs to describe properties of the file. For instance, files ending in COM, BAT, and EXE are programs that can be run. Files ending in TXT are usually text files, often containing information of interest. (Later you'll see how to read these and similar files.)

Getting Down to Work

Now that you know enough to be dangerous, let's put some of that know-how to work in Lesson 3. You'll learn how to run some popular programs.

Running Programs

3

Oh good. You're still here. When you want to use a program (WordPerfect, or Quicken, or whatever), you must tell DOS that you want to use it by *running* the program. I have a pleasant surprise. If you did the work in the last two lessons, you already know how to run at least one program—DOSSHELL.COM. When you typed DOSSHELL at the DOS prompt, you ran it.

You can run files that end with extensions like COM, EXE, and BAT by simply typing their names at the DOS prompt—you don't even need to type the extension. As you've already seen, DOSSHELL is the same as DOSSHELL.COM, as far as DOS is concerned. So's dosshell, for that matter. All executable files run when you type their names at the DOS prompt. So why a whole lesson on *this* topic?

Not so fast. DOS needs to know a few things to work reliably under different circumstances.

Details, Details, Details

Today, once a program is properly installed on your hard disk, to run it you need to know the following:

- If the program needs Microsoft Windows

- The name of the program file itself

- Where the program is located (the path)

- If you want to use a mouse to start the program

Let's take 'em one at a time.

Does the Program Require Windows?

Some programs are designed to run both with and without Windows; others need Windows to run. Some won't run with Windows at all. Which do you have? I honestly don't know. A few of each, I'd bet. Sometimes a program's name holds important clues—*Word for Windows* is a dead giveaway, for instance. Other times, you'll need to read the box—or (gasp) the documentation that came with the program. You *bought* all those programs, right?

Other times you may need to ask a guru, or even call the program's maker to see if the program will (or must) run under Windows.

What's the Program's File Name?

Next you'll need to know the *name* of the executable file. Here are some common file names for popular non-Windows programs (notice we've left off the unnecessary file-name extensions):

PROGRAM NAME	FILE NAME
dBASE	dbase
Flight Simulator	fs
Harvard Graphics	hg
LapLink	ll
Lotus 1-2-3	123
Managing Your Money	mym
Microsoft Word (non-Windows versions)	word

PROGRAM NAME	FILE NAME
MultiMate	wp
PageMaker	pm
PROCOMM Plus	pcplus
Prodigy	prodigy
Q&A	qa
Quattro	q
Quicken	q (yep, a duplicate!)
Ventura Publisher	vp
WordPerfect (non-Windows versions)	wp
WordStar	ws

And here are the file names for some popular Windows programs:

PROGRAM	FILE NAME
FileMaker Pro for Windows	fmpro
Microsoft Excel	excel
Microsoft Money	msmoney
Microsoft PowerPoint	powerpnt
Microsoft Windows	win
Microsoft Word for Windows	word
Microsoft Works for Windows	winworks
PageMaker for Windows	pm
WordPerfect for Windows	wpwin

Where the Heck Is It?

Many new programs install themselves in their own brand-new, nice, neat subdirectories, which are obvious and well documented. Other times it's left up to the owner to decide where to put the programs. Some folks just dump them all into the hard drive's root directory, a guarantee of trouble sooner or later.

Again, the program's manuals will often tell you the name of the subdirectory containing the program.

Or, you could use the DOS Shell and other tools described in later lessons to locate the lost program. But we are getting ahead of ourselves.

● Note Sometimes DOS knows where to look for a file, even if you don't, thanks to a thing called a path in your AUTOEXEC.BAT file, discussed in Lesson 18. If you don't know the program's location, try running it from the DOS prompt anyway. You might get lucky.

To Point and Click, or to Type?

The final thing to know is if you plan to use a mouse to start up your program. If you like your mouse, use it with the DOS Shell or Windows to start the program. If you hate your mouse or don't have one, forget the DOS Shell (and Windows, if possible). Use the plain-old DOS prompt instead.

Armed with the name and location of the program, the knowledge that it does—or does *not*—require Windows, and your feelings toward mice, you can take a stab at running it. Obviously, this assumes that the program has been properly installed on your computer and that the computer has the required bells and whistles to run it.

Running Non-Windows Programs from the Shell

Let's start by running a program you almost certainly have. It's called **EDIT.COM** and is located in your hard disk's **DOS** subdirectory on your **C:** drive. (It is normally placed there by the DOS 6 installation routine.) EDIT.COM is a little word-processing program that is handy to have, as you will see in later lessons. It does *not* need Windows.

Oh, yes. If you don't have a mouse, skip ahead to the section titled "Running Non-Windows Programs from the DOS Prompt."

Are they gone? OK, mousketeers, if the Shell is not running, run it (type **DOSSHELL** at the DOS prompt).

1. Make sure the **C:** drive is the active drive. The disk icon should be darker than the rest, and the letter C should be highlighted. Point and click with your mouse, if necessary, to select drive C.

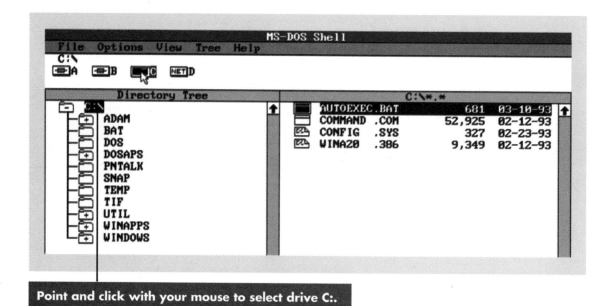

Point and click with your mouse to select drive C:.

2. Choose the **DOS** subdirectory by pointing and clicking, this time on the DOS folder. Your screen should look like this:

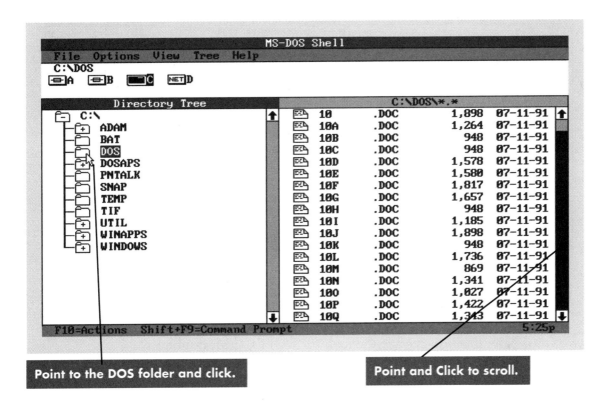

Point to the DOS folder and click.

Point and Click to scroll.

3. Next, find the file **EDIT.COM** in the file list on the right side of the screen. You'll need to scroll to see it. Do this by pointing to and clicking on the scroll bar at the right edge of the screen. Clicking below the rectangular "elevator box" (called the scroll, or slider, box) moves you down in the list. Clicking above it moves you back up. For this exercise, you'll probably need to move down.

Quick&Easy

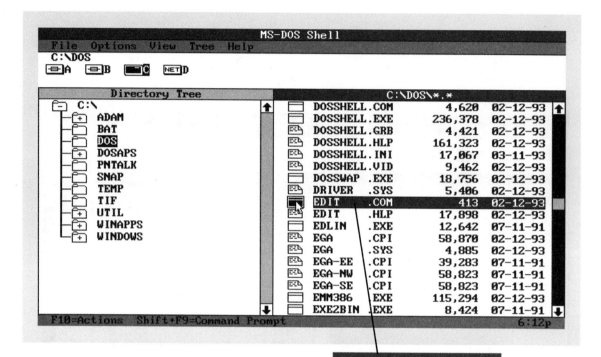

Here's the **EDIT.COM** file.

4. Now that you can see the icon for EDIT.COM, double-click on it (point to the icon, then press and release the left mouse button twice in rapid succession). Double clicking takes some practice. Try again if nothing happens at first.

Soon the Shell will run the EDIT program for you. Your screen should look like this:

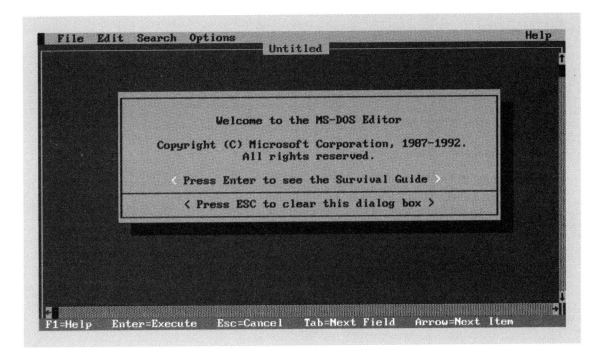

```
 File  Edit  Search  Options                                      Help
                              Untitled
```

```
              Welcome to the MS-DOS Editor

        Copyright (C) Microsoft Corporation, 1987-1992.
                  All rights reserved.

          < Press Enter to see the Survival Guide >

          < Press ESC to clear this dialog box >
```

```
F1=Help    Enter=Execute    Esc=Cancel    Tab=Next Field    Arrow=Next Item
```

5. Let's quit the program now and return to the Shell. You'll learn more about EDIT later. Every program quits a little differently. To quit EDIT, press Escape (sometimes labeled Esc—you can find it in the upper-left corner of your keyboard). Then point to the File option and press the mouse button to display the menu.

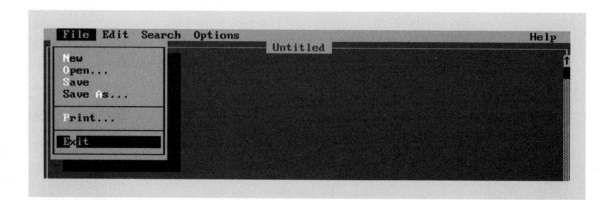

6. Click on the **Exit** choice to quit running the EDIT program. You'll see a message inviting you back to the Shell (if
EDIT asks if you want to save anything, click on the No
button).

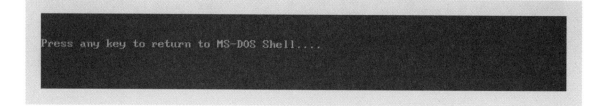

7. You can press *nearly* any key to get back. Shift, Ctrl, and a
few others won't work, but the spacebar sure does. Hit it!

Running Non-Windows Programs
from the DOS Prompt

No mouse, hey? No matter. (Mouseketeers will want to try this exercise
too.) We'll run HELP.COM, one of the DOS 6 Help programs, by using the DOS prompt.

Quit the Shell if it is running (press the Shift-F9 key combination), then try running the HELP.COM program at the prompt:

1. At the DOS prompt, type this complete path name and file name:

C:\DOS\HELP.COM

```
C:\>C:\DOS\HELP.COM
```

● Note When running programs from the DOS prompt, you can often leave out things like the drive letter or even the path name, and you can always leave out a program's file extension when running programs. For instance, the command *help* all by itself would probably work just fine in step 1. But if you have two programs with identical file names in different directories on your disk (Quicken and Quattro, for instance, both have the file name Q.EXE), DOS might run the wrong program if you don't include the path name. So, to be safe and unambiguous, type everything, at least until you understand the implications of shorthand entries.

---

2. Press ↵. Shortly after you press the Enter key, you'll see a screen like this, indicating that the program has run successfully:

```
 File   Search                                                    Help
                        MS-DOS Help: Command Reference
 Use the scroll bars to see more commands. Or, press the PAGE DOWN key. For
 more information about using MS-DOS Help, choose How to Use MS-DOS Help
 from the Help menu, or press F1. To exit MS-DOS Help, press ALT, F, X.

 <ANSI.SYS>                  <Erase>                 <Multi-config>
 <Append>                    <Exit>                  <Nlsfunc>
 <Attrib>                    <Expand>                <Numlock>
 <Batch commands>            <Fasthelp>              <Path>
 <Break>                     <Fastopen>              <Pause>
 <Buffers>                   <Fc>                    <Power>
 <Call>                      <Fcbs>                  <POWER.EXE>
 <Cd>                        <Fdisk>                 <Print>
 <Chcp>                      <Files>                 <Prompt>
 <Chdir>                     <Find>                  <Qbasic>
 <Chkdsk>                    <For>                   <RAMDRIVE.SYS>
 <CHKSTATE.SYS>              <Format>                <Rd>
 <Choice>                    <Goto>                  <Rem>
 <Cls>                       <Graphics>              <Ren>
 <Command>                   <Help>                  <Rename>
 <CONFIG.SYS commands>       <HIMEM.SYS>             <Replace>
 <Copy>                      <If>                    <Restore>
 <Alt+C=Contents> <Alt+N=Next> <Alt+B=Back>               C   00006:002
```

You are looking at a list of DOS commands. The Help program can
tell you a few things about each of them. You'll learn more about DOS
Help features in Lesson 14, but if you are curious, you can't hurt anything by poking around these self-explanatory screens. The trick is to
move the cursor under a command you want to know about, then
press ↵. Just read all the on-screen instructions and pay attention to the
ever-changing choices at the bottom of your display. Most of this command help is in shorthand for techies, so don't be put off by the com-
plexity of what you'll read here.

3. When you are finished with HELP.COM, press **Alt-F** and
then **X** to quit the program.

About Start-up Options, or Switches

Some programs let you type additional information at the DOS
prompt that may be useful. For instance, when starting WordPerfect,
instead of just typing **wp**, you could include the name of a document

you wish to work on. The document will appear on your screen when WordPerfect starts.

Other programs like Q&A let you specify oddball display types and colors (for portables and such), if you type extra characters after the program's file name. And HELP.COM will scoot right to information about a particular command if you type the command name after the program name (try **HELP DIR**, for instance). Pretty slick! Check your documentation to see what options are available at start-up.

Running Windows from the DOS Prompt

Running Windows itself from the DOS prompt is pretty simple. Just type **win** and press ↵ at the DOS prompt:

```
C:\>win
```

● Note If you always work in Windows, you can have DOS start Windows for you each time you turn on your computer. You do this by adding the command *win* to your AUTOEXEC.BAT file (this file is described in Lesson 17).

If you use Windows frequently, you probably know at least one of the several ways to run Windows programs from within Windows. Just double-click on the icon for the desired program in Program Manager. (For details, you'll want to check out *Windows Quick & Easy*, by Robert Cowart, SYBEX, 1992.)

20 MINUTES

LESSON 4

Viewing the Contents and Organization of Your Disks

There are four different ways to see what's on a disk: You can use the DOS Shell, the DOS Directory command (DIR), the DOS TREE command (TREE), or the Windows File Manager (if you have Windows on your machine). Let's take a look at the DOS techniques.

Using the Shell to View a Disk's Contents

While running the DOS Shell you can poke around with your mouse to view a disk's contents and organization. With the DOS Shell running:

1. Click on the icon of the desired drive—**C**: for this exercise. Clicking on an icon selects the corresponding drive and displays the contents of its root directory. A selected drive's icon will look different from the others (notice drive C in the example).

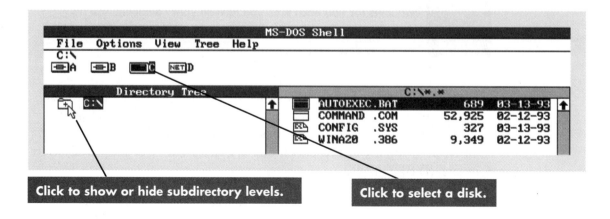

Click to show or hide subdirectory levels.

Click to select a disk.

32

2. Next, click once on a folder, if necessary, to display its contents. The root directory's folder is selected in the example. (Normally, when you select a drive, its root directory is automatically displayed for you.) A folder displaying a + has "hidden" contents—files and/or additional subdirectories, which you can reveal by clicking on the folder. Clicking multiple times on the same folder alternately shows and hides subdirectories. Try this a few times until it makes sense. When you are done experimenting, display the contents of your root directory, and select your DOS folder by pointing and clicking once on your DOS folder icon, as shown here:

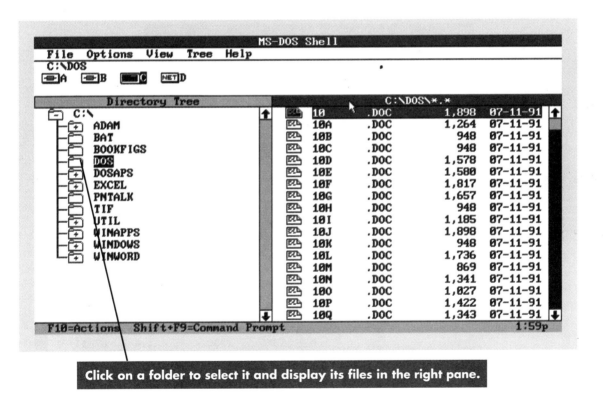

Click on a folder to select it and display its files in the right pane.

Do you see how the DOS subdirectory's name is highlighted in the example and on your screen? That means you are looking at the DOS subdirectory. Notice that the Shell window consists of left and right sides, or *panes*. The left pane displays folders (subdirectories), and the right pane shows the files, if any, contained in a selected subdirectory. Notice also that the path and display options are displayed along the top of the file-list pane (C:\DOS*.* in this example).

3. Your DOS subdirectory has so many files that you'll need to scroll to see them all. But before you can scroll, you'll need to activate the file list (the right pane). Press the **Tab** key or point and click on the bar at the top of the file list. Notice how the top of the bar changes color (or darkens) when you've activated its corresponding pane. Each time you press **Tab** the other pane is activated.

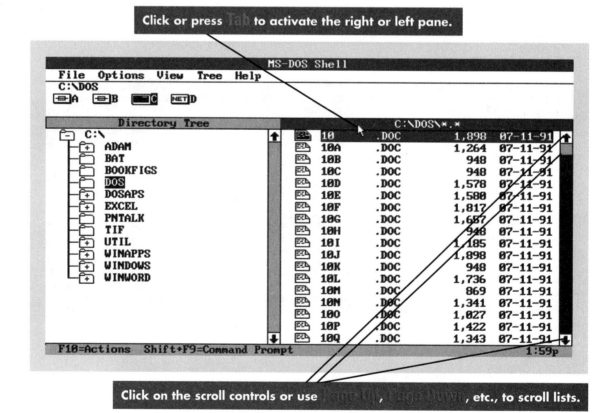

Click or press Tab to activate the right or left pane.

Click on the scroll controls or use Page Up, Page Down, etc., to scroll lists.

4. To scroll through a long list of files or subdirectories, you can use your mouse or various keyboard shortcuts. To scroll with your mouse, point and click on the scroll bars at the right of the activated pane. You'll probably find the keyboard shortcuts quicker, particularly in long lists. Page Up, Page Down, Home, and End all work as you'd expect. Give them a try.

> **● Note** Typing the first letter of a name in a file list takes you to the first entry that begins with that letter. Pressing P, for instance, might take you to PACKING.LST, pressing P again might take you to PMENU.DOC, and so on. This trick also works in the directory pane, where typing a letter takes you to folders (subdirectories) that start with the letter (D for DOS DELUXE, DRV, DOS, and so on).

Viewing the Contents of Floppies

Look at directories and files on floppies just as you would on the hard disk. Click on the appropriate disk icon (**A:** or **B:**) to select it. Just make sure there is a floppy in drive A: or B: before you click or DOS will scold you.

Seeing Greater or Lesser Detail

There are many ways to increase or decrease the amount of detail shown on your screen. For instance, the Expand All choice on the Shell's Tree menu lets you see all your subdirectories so that you can easily get "the big picture." Compare the expanded illustration that follows with the previous one, then try expanding your view.

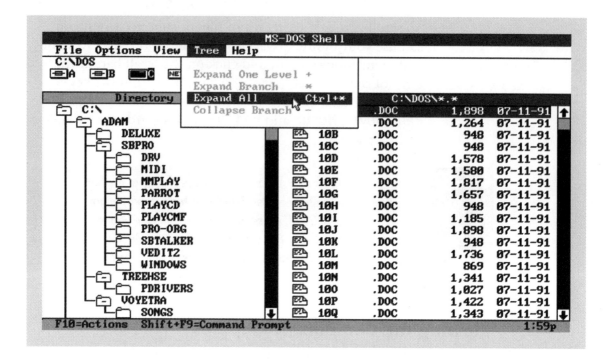

1. Choose **Expand All** from the Shell's Tree menu.

2. Activate the directory (left) pane by pointing or tabbing if necessary.

3. Scroll through the resulting subdirectory list in the left pane by pointing and clicking on the scroll tools or by using the keyboard shortcuts, like **Page Up**, **Page Down**, etc.

4. The **Collapse Branch** choice on the Shell's Tree menu hides subdirectories. Experiment with the other two Expand commands (**Expand One Level** and **Expand Branch**) if you wish, to see how they work too.

Another option is to use the All Files choice (on the Shell's View menu). It lists all the files on the selected disk, alphabetically or in other orders that you specify. You can select a single file by pointing and clicking (the up and down arrow keys work here too), then learn the file's characteristics (size, creation date, location, and so on).

In this example, you can see the information for the EDIT.COM file:

Select a file here.

```
                          MS-DOS Shell
  File  Options  View  Tree  Help
  C:\DOS
  ⊟A  ⊟B  ■C  NET⌐D
                                        *.*
                        DS_2400  .SCR    2,552  07-09-90  12:00p
  File                  DS_24MNP .SCR    2,299  07-09-90  12:00p
    Name  : EDIT.COM    DS_HAYES .SCR    2,552  07-09-90  12:00p
    Attr  : ...a        DS_HAYSV .SCR    2,299  07-09-90  12:00p
  Selected        C     DS_TBIT  .SCR    2,299  07-09-90  12:00p
    Number:       1     DISK     .XLS    2,163  04-01-92  12:00p
    Size  :     413     DXFIMP   .FLT    3,392  08-08-91   5:48p
  Directory             EDISON   .DOC    1,819  06-04-92   1:24p
    Name  : DOS         EDIT     .COM      413  02-12-93   6:00a
    Size  : 5,356,449   EDIT     .HLP   17,898  02-12-93   6:00a
    Files :     207     EDLIN    .EXE   12,642  07-11-91   6:00p
  Disk                  EEPUTV13 .EXE   52,796  01-11-93  12:35p
    Name  : AST_RON'S   EGA      .CPI   58,870  02-12-93   6:00a
    Size  : 120,971,264 EGA      .SYS    4,885  02-12-93   6:00a
    Avail : 23,021,568  EGA-EE   .CPI   39,283  07-11-91   6:00p
    Files :   1,498     EGA-NW   .CPI   58,823  07-11-91   6:00p
    Dirs  :      87     EGA-SE   .CPI   58,823  07-11-91   6:00p
                        EGA40WOA .FON    8,368  03-10-92   3:10a
  F10=Actions  Shift+F9=Command Prompt                    3:53p
```

Read about the file here.

To try the Single File feature yourself:

1. Point and click to select the disk you want to look at (C:, for instance).

2. Choose **All Files** from the Shell's View menu.

3. Point and click in the resulting file list to select a file of interest (scroll if necessary, and select using any of the keyboard tricks you learned earlier).

4. Read about the selected file.

5. Select Single File List or another menu choice to leave the All Files view when you are done.

Notice that while in All Files view, there are a number of statistics listed on the left side of the screen. For instance, you can see which subdirectory contains the selected file, the total number of files in that subdirectory, the amount of disk space used by all files in that subdirectory, and so on.

Getting Information about Multiple Files

Suppose you want to copy several files to a floppy disk and wonder if they will all fit on one disk. You can use the All Files view to "add up" the file space required. Do this by selecting multiple files in the list. You select a range of contiguous files in a list by pointing and clicking on the first file, then holding down the Shift key while pointing to the last file in the range.

For instance, in the preceding example, to select all files between and including EDIT.COM and EDLIN.EXE, you could

1. Point to EDIT.COM and click.

2. Hold down the Shift key, then point and click on EDLIN.EXE.

Click here.

```
File                          DS_24MNP .SCR    2,299  07-09-90  12:00p
  Name  : EDIT.COM            DS_HAYES .SCR    2,552  07-09-90  12:00p
  Attr  : ...a                DS_HAYSV .SCR    2,299  07-09-90  12:00p
Selected         C            DS_TBIT  .SCR    2,299  07-09-90  12:00p
  Number:        3            DUSK     .XLS    2,163  04-01-92  12:00p
  Size  :   30,953            DXFIMP   .FLT    3,392  08-08-91   5:48p
Directory                     EDISON   .DOC    1,819  06-04-92   1:24p
  Name  : DOS                 EDIT     .COM      413  02-12-93   6:00a
  Size  : 5,356,445           EDIT     .HLP   17,898  02-12-93   6:00a
  Files :      207            EDLIN    .EXE   12,642  07-11-91   6:00p
Disk                          EEPUTV13.EXE    52,796  01-11-93  12:35p
  Name  : AST_RON'S           EGA      .CPI   58,870  02-12-93   6:00a
  Size  : 120,971,264         EGA      .SYS    4,885  02-12-93   6:00a
  Avail : 22,794,240          EGA-EE   .CPI   39,283  07-11-91   6:00p
  Files :    1,502            EGA-NW   .CPI   58,823  07-11-91   6:00p
  Dirs  :       87            EGA-SE   .CPI   58,823  07-11-91   6:00p
                              EGA40WOA.FON     8,368  03-10-92   3:10a
 F10=Actions  Shift+F9=Command Prompt                          10:24a
```

Hold down the Shift key and click here.
Files in between will also be selected.

EDLIN.COM, EDLIN.HLP, and EDLIN.EXE are all highlighted, indicating they have been selected. The statistics at the left of the screen reflect the totals for all selected files.

Here's another handy shortcut: To select noncontiguous items in a list (EDIT.COM and EDLIN.EXE but not EDIT.HLP, for instance), hold down the **Ctrl** key and click on individual file names. Just the files you Control-click on will be selected. Control-clicking on a file name a second time deselects it.

Getting File Information in Other Views

You can get similar file information in other views (like the Single File List view). Use the Show Information... command on the Shell's Options menu:

1. Select the file you want information on (point and click or use the arrow keys).

2. Choose **Show Information**... from the Shell's Options menu.

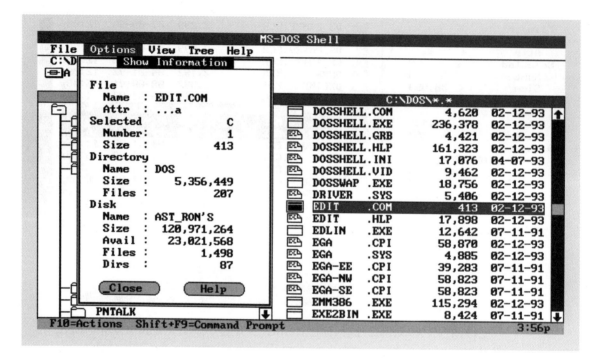

3. Read the file information.

4. Press **Escape** or click the Close button when finished.

Changing the Order of File Lists

File-name lists are normally displayed alphabetically, but you can view them arranged by ascending or descending extension, last modified date, or disk order.

1. Display a file list using any of the techniques previously described.

2. Choose **File Display Options**... from the Shell's Options menu. You'll see the File Display Options dialog box:

See Lesson 5 for details.

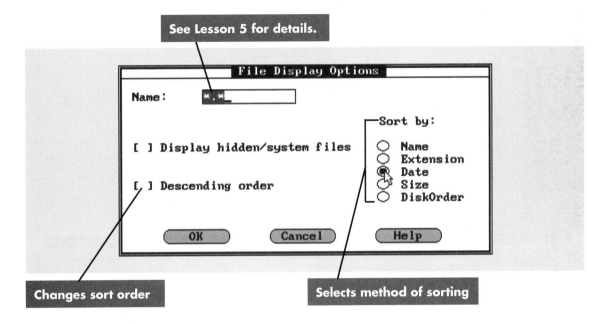

Changes sort order

Selects method of sorting

3. Pick the desired options from the dialog box. For instance, to display files by date, click on the Date button. To display them in descending date order (most recently modified files first), click between the [ ] next to the Descending order choice.

4. After making your file display option choices, click on the OK button to reorder the file list.

● **Note** You can also limit the types of files displayed by using things called wildcards. That's the purpose of the mysterious-looking Name: entry area containing the *.* in the preceding illustration. You'll learn about wildcards in the next lesson.

Viewing Two Disks or Subdirectories at a Time

There are times when it is helpful to view the contents of two disks at once. For instance, you may wish to compare the modification dates of two files on different disks, or you might want to copy a file from one disk to another, or you may want to look at two different directories on

the same disk simultaneously. The Shell's Dual File Lists choice on the
View menu makes these tasks easier.

1. Insert a floppy or floppies, if necessary.

2. Choose Dual File Lists from the Shell's View menu.

3. Click or press **Tab** to select the disks and directories of interest in the resulting split-screen view.

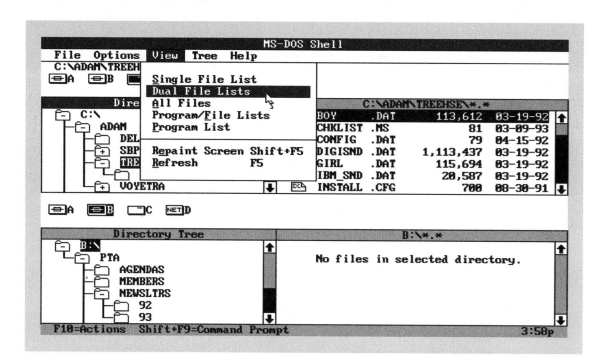

4. Work in either the top or bottom half of the screen normally.

Using the DOS DIR Command to View a Disk's Contents

Now that you've seen how to explore your disk with the Shell's graphical whizbangs, you may never want to use the old DOS directory command (DIR). But here's how it works, just in case.

The unembellished DIR command will list all the files in the current subdirectory of the current disk. It also shows each file's size in bytes, the date and time of last modification, and totals for files listed and the disk's remaining free space. If there are more files than will fit on the screen, the file names will scroll past, and you'll see the last files listed when the scrolling stops.

Try it. At the DOS prompt, simply type

        DIR \DOS

and press ↵:

```
C:\>dir \dos
```

You'll see a list of the files in your DOS subdirectory. Since there are too many files to fit on your screen, you'll just see the last part of the list. There are additional switches you can use with the DIR prompt to overcome this problem.

```
SIZER      EXE       7169 02-12-93   6:00a
MONOUMB    386       8783 02-12-93   6:00a
MSTOOLS    DLL      13424 02-12-93   6:00a
MSAVIRUS   LST      35520 02-12-93   6:00a
VSAFE      COM      62576 02-12-93   6:00a
MWAVDOSL   DLL      44736 02-12-93   6:00a
MWAVDRVL   DLL       7744 02-12-93   6:00a
MWAVDLG    DLL      36368 02-12-93   6:00a
MWAVSCAN   DLL     151568 02-12-93   6:00a
MWAV       EXE     142640 02-12-93   6:00a
MWAVABSI   DLL      54576 02-12-93   6:00a
MWAV       HLP      25663 02-12-93   6:00a
MWAVSOS    DLL       7888 02-12-93   6:00a
MWAVMGR    DLL      21712 02-12-93   6:00a
MWAVTSR    EXE      17328 02-12-93   6:00a
COMMAND    COM      52925 02-12-93   6:00a
CHKLIST    MS        2700 03-09-93   4:16p
MWAV       INI         24 03-09-93   4:19p
CONFIG     UMB        236 02-19-93  12:38p
MEMMAKER   STS        999 02-22-93   4:45p
DOSSHELL   INI      17070 04-10-93  11:25a
       210 file(s)    5356468 bytes
                     22691840 bytes free

C:\>
```

Useful DIR Command Switches

By adding the switch /P to the DIR command, DOS will fill the
screen with files, pause for you to read them, and refill the screen with
new files when you press most any key (the spacebar, for instance). The
result of the command DIR \DOS /P is shown here. Notice the
prompt "Press any key to continue."

```
COUNTRY    SYS      17066 02-12-93   6:00a
EGA-EE     CPI      39283 07-11-91   6:00p
EGA-NW     CPI      58823 07-11-91   6:00p
EGA-SE     CPI      58823 07-11-91   6:00p
KEYB       COM      14983 02-12-93   6:00a
KEYBOARD   SYS      34694 02-12-93   6:00a
ANSI       SYS       9065 02-12-93   6:00a
ATTRIB     EXE      11165 02-12-93   6:00a
CHKDSK     EXE      12908 02-12-93   6:00a
EDIT       COM        413 02-12-93   6:00a
EXPAND     EXE      16129 02-12-93   6:00a
Press any key to continue . . .
```

If you can live without file size, creation date, and other file info, the /W switch lets you see more file names on the screen by providing a "wide," or columnar, view of files. Here's the result of the command DIR /DOS /W:

```
LOADFIX.COM      MWBACKUP.EXE    MWBACKUP.HLP     REPLACE.EXE      SUBST.EXE
TREE.COM         DOSKEY.COM      VFINTD.386       MWBACKF.DLL      MWBACKR.DLL
CHKSTATE.SYS     UNDELETE.EXE    MWUNDEL.EXE      MWUNDEL.HLP      MWGRAFIC.DLL
WNTOOLS.GRP      MEMMAKER.HLP    MEMMAKER.INF     INTERLNK.EXE     INTERSVR.EXE
DBLSPACE.EXE     MSCDEX.EXE      DBLSPACE.HLP     DBLSPACE.INF     DBLSPACE.SYS
DBLWIN.HLP       DOSSHELL.HLP    EMM386.EXE       MEMMAKER.EXE     SIZER.EXE
MONOUMB.386      MSTOOLS.DLL     MSAVIRUS.LST     VSAFE.COM        MWAVDOSL.DLL
MWAVDRVL.DLL     MWAVDLG.DLL     MWAVSCAN.DLL     MWAV.EXE         MWAVABSI.DLL
MWAV.HLP         MWAVSOS.DLL     MWAVMGR.DLL      MWAVTSR.EXE      COMMAND.COM
CHKLIST.MS       MWAV.INI        CONFIG.UMB       MEMMAKER.STS     DOSSHELL.INI
       210 file(s)        5356468 bytes
                         22669312 bytes free

C:\>
```

You can force DOS to list files in alphabetical order, if you like, with the sort order, or /O, switch. The "plain" /O switch lists files by file name in ascending alphabetical order. The figure on the following page illustrates how the result of the command DIR \DOS /O looks on my machine (it shows the bottom of the file list).

```
REMLINE  BAS      12314 07-11-91    6:00p
REPLACE  EXE      20226 02-12-93    6:00a
RESTORE  EXE      38294 02-12-93    6:00a
RMENU    DOC       1898 07-11-91    6:00p
SETVER   EXE      12015 02-23-93    3:07p
SHARE    EXE      10912 02-12-93    6:00a
SIZER    EXE       7169 02-12-93    6:00a
SMARTDRV EXE      42073 02-12-93    6:00a
SMARTDRV SYS       8335 07-11-91    6:00p
SMARTMON EXE      28672 02-12-93    6:00a
SMARTMON HLP      10727 02-12-93    6:00a
SORT     EXE       6922 02-12-93    6:00a
SUBST    EXE      18478 02-12-93    6:00a
SYS      COM       9379 02-12-93    6:00a
TREE     COM       6898 02-12-93    6:00a
UNDELETE EXE      26420 02-12-93    6:00a
UNFORMAT COM      12738 02-12-93    6:00a
VFINTD   386       5295 02-12-93    6:00a
VSAFE    COM      62576 02-12-93    6:00a
WNTOOLS  GRP       2205 04-10-93   12:11p
XCOPY    EXE      15820 02-12-93    6:00a
       210 file(s)     5356468 bytes
                      22620160 bytes free

C:\>
```

There are various flavors of the sort-order switch as well. For instance, you can sort by date, size, and so on.

 Note To learn more about the DOS prompt and its switches, use the HELP DIR command. It will show you the available DIR options and examples of their use.

And, yes, switches can be combined. There is no need to separate each switch with a space, but you do need to include a slash between each switch. For instance, here's what happens when I type **DIR \DOS /W/O/P** on my machine, requesting a wide list of the contents of my DOS directory sorted by name. Try this on your own machine.

```
Volume in drive C is AST_RON'S
Volume Serial Number is 1A57-78F1
Directory of C:\DOS

[.]           [..]          10.DOC        10A.DOC       10B.DOC
10C.DOC       10D.DOC       10E.DOC       10F.DOC       10G.DOC
10H.DOC       10I.DOC       10J.DOC       10K.DOC       10L.DOC
10M.DOC       10N.DOC       10O.DOC       10P.DOC       10Q.DOC
10R.DOC       10S.DOC       10T.DOC       10U.DOC       1A.DOC
1B.DOC        2.DOC         2A.DOC        2B.DOC        2B0DDOSC.BAT
2C.DOC        2D.DOC        2D2.DOC       2D3.DOC       2E.DOC
2F.DOC        3A.DOC        3B.DOC        4.DOC         4201.CPI
4208.CPI      4A.DOC        4B.DOC        5.DOC         5202.CPI
5A.DOC        5B.DOC        5C.DOC        5D.DOC        5E.DOC
6.DOC         6A.DOC        6B.DOC        6C.DOC        7.DOC
7A.DOC        7B.DOC        7C.DOC        7D.DOC        8A.DOC
8B.DOC        8C.DOC        9A.DOC        9B.DOC        ANSI.SYS
APPEND.EXE    ASSIGN.COM    ATTRIB.EXE    AUTOEXEC.UMB  CHKDSK.EXE
CHKLIST.MS    CHKSTATE.SYS  CHOICE.COM    COMMAND.COM   COMP.EXE
CONFIG.UMB    COUNTR50.SYS  COUNTRY.SYS   DBLSPACE.BIN  DBLSPACE.EXE
DBLSPACE.HLP  DBLSPACE.INF  DBLSPACE.SYS  DBLWIN.HLP    DEBUG.EXE
DEFRAG.EXE    DEFRAG.HLP    DELOLDOS.EXE  DELTREE.EXE   DISKCOMP.COM
DISKCOPY.COM  DISPLAY.SYS   DOSHELP.HLP   DOSKEY.COM    DOSSHELL.COM
Press any key to continue . . .
```

Using the DOS TREE Command

The DOS TREE command lets you see a graphical representation of your disk's subdirectories and optionally, the files contained in each subdirectory. Since most hard disks have more subdirectories than can be displayed on the screen at once, and since the /P switch does not work with the TREE command, you'll want to get in the habit of using another screen-controlling feature, called the *More pipe*. Here's how to use the TREE prompt with the More pipe:

1. Type **TREE** | more and press ↵. (You need to separate the command TREE and the word *more* with a |, sometimes called the stick character or vertical bar. Spaces are optional.)

You will see the first part of the current disk's subdirectory organization. Then the computer will pause.

```
Directory PATH listing for Volume AST_RON'S
Volume Serial Number is 1A57-78F1
C:.
├───TIF
├───BAT
├───DOS
├───ADAM
│   ├───DELUXE
│   ├───TREEHSE
│   │   └───PDRIVERS
│   ├───VOYETRA
│   │   └───SONGS
│   └───SBPRO
│       ├───DRV
│       ├───PRO-ORG
│       ├───PLAYCD
│       ├───PLAYCMF
│       ├───VEDIT2
│       ├───SBTALKER
│       ├───PARROT
│       ├───MMPLAY
│       ├───WINDOWS
│       └───MIDI
-- More --
```

2. Press nearly any key (perhaps the spacebar) to see more of the tree.

3. Continue reading and pressing any key until you've seen the whole disk organization or press Ctrl-C to abort the tree display.

Useful TREE Switches

You can include a drive name in your command (TREE B: | more, for instance). Or, to restrict a tree display to a particular subdirectory, include its name in the command. For instance, TREE C:\WINAPPS only displays subdirectories within the WINAPPS subdirectory.

To include *file names* in the tree display, add the switch /F. Thus, the command TREE C:\WINAPPS /F | more lists all the subdirectories *and files* found in the WINAPPS subdirectory on drive C.

```
┌─FMPRO
│       CLARISTB.DLL
│       CLARISMM.DLL
│       LOG.TXT
│       README.WRI
│       APPLENW.DLL
│       CLARISNW.DLL
│       FMPNTALK.EXE
│       FMPRO.EXE
│       FMPRO.HLP
│       CHKLIST.MS
│
├──TUTORIAL
│       CATALOG.FM
│       EMPLNUMS.FM
│       EMPLOYEE.FM
│       PRODUCTS.FM
│       SALES.FM
│       FOTO.PCX
│       LOGO.PCX
│
└────TEMPLATE
        CONTACTS.FM
── More ──
```

Printing File and Subdirectory Lists

To print the results of DIR and TREE commands, add the PRN pipe to your commands. (Remember, "PRN pipe" just means that you're telling DOS to redirect the output of the DIR command to your printer.) For instance, DIR > PRN prints a list of the files in your current subdirectory to your printer, TREE C:\WINAPPS /F > PRN prints a "graphical" list of subdirectories and files contained in the WINAPPS subdirectory, and so forth. Make sure your printer is turned on and ready before attempting this.

Using Windows to View a Disk's Contents

If you have Windows on your machine, you may want to use the File Manager to view the contents of your disks. It has all the features found in the DOS Shell and more. Run File Manager from the Program Manager. Many people set up Windows to automatically run File Manager at start-up.

LESSON 5

Wildcards—Saving Time and Your Eyesight 5

W ildcards are tools that DOS uses to help you deal with multiple files at the same time. They are most useful at the DOS prompt, but they can also be used in the Shell and with Windows. The two DOS wildcard characters are the asterisk (*) and the question mark (?). Since it's easiest to see the usefulness of wildcards at the DOS prompt, let's start there.

Using Wildcards to Find Selected Files

Suppose that you know there are some files in your DOS subdirectory that end with the extension .TXT, and you want to see a list of them. You *could* use the DIR command with the PAUSE switch (/P) to look at every file in the DOS subdirectory until you found all the files ending with the extension TXT, but the asterisk wildcard can make the task much easier. Try this:

1. Quit the Shell or Windows if necessary and get to the DOS prompt.

2. Switch to the DOS subdirectory by typing CD\DOS and pressing ↵.

3. Type the command DIR *.TXT and press ↵.

You should see just a list of files in the DOS subdirectory that end with the TXT extension:

```
C:\>cd\dos

C:\DOS>dir *.txt

 Volume in drive C is AST_RON'S
 Volume Serial Number is 1A57-78F1
 Directory of C:\DOS

NETWORKS TXT      21450 02-12-93    6:00a
README   TXT      57349 02-12-93    6:00a
        2 file(s)        78799 bytes
                      22587392 bytes free

C:\DOS>
```

When you use the asterisk wildcard this way, you are saying to DOS, "Show me every file name that ends with the extension TXT." You can use the asterisk for *parts* of file names and in *file-name extensions* as well. For instance, you could find all files that *begin* with the letter H and end in any extension:

1. Quit the Shell or Windows if necessary and get to the DOS prompt.

2. If necessary, switch to the DOS subdirectory by typing CD\DOS and pressing ↵.

3. Type the command DIR H*.* and press ↵.

You should see just a list of files in the DOS subdirectory that
start with the letter H, regardless of their extensions:

```
C:\DOS>dir h*.*

 Volume in drive C is AST_RON'S
 Volume Serial Number is 1A57-78F1
 Directory of C:\DOS

HIMEM    SYS     14224 02-12-93   6:00a
HELP     HLP    294741 02-12-93   6:00a
HELP     COM       413 02-12-93   6:00a
        3 file(s)      309378 bytes
                     22558720 bytes free

C:\DOS>
```

As you can see, this trick lists all files beginning with the letter H regardless of their extensions.

Using Wildcards to List Subdirectories

Have you ever forgotten the exact name of a subdirectory or wished
you could get a quick list of all of them? Here's one way to do that at
the DOS prompt. Since subdirectories don't have extensions, using a
wildcard to ask for a list of file names that don't contain extensions will
show you subdirectories. Try it:

1. Quit the Shell or Windows if necessary and get to the DOS
   prompt.

2. Switch to the root (or another directory of interest) by typing CD followed by the directory name or path, and pressing ↵. (CD\ takes you to the root directory, for instance.)

3. Type the command DIR *. and press ↵. Notice that you do
   not type a second asterisk after the period!

You should see just a list of files in the subdirectory that do not have file extensions. The items with <DIR> are all subdirectories.

```
C:\>dir *.

 Volume in drive C is AST_RON'S
 Volume Serial Number is 1A57-78F1
 Directory of C:\

TIF          <DIR>      03-09-93    6:29p
BAT          <DIR>      03-09-93    6:30p
DOS          <DIR>      01-08-92   10:35a
ADAM         <DIR>      03-09-93    6:36p
UTIL         <DIR>      01-08-92   10:36a
WINDOWS      <DIR>      01-08-92   10:36a
WINAPPS      <DIR>      01-08-92   10:38a
DOSAPS       <DIR>      03-10-93    9:25a
MT           <DIR>      04-07-93    2:36p
BOOKFIGS     <DIR>      03-12-93    9:21a
EXCEL        <DIR>      03-12-93   10:18a
PNTALK       <DIR>      03-18-92    4:43p
WINWORD      <DIR>      03-12-93   10:19a
IMAFILE               3 04-12-93    2:46p
       14 file(s)              3 bytes
                        22542336 bytes free

C:\>
```

If the subdirectory you are exploring contains *files* that don't have any extensions, those files will be listed along with the subdirectories. For instance, there is one file (called IMAFILE) in the example. The rest are all subdirectories and are easily spotted by the <DIR> notation after their names and the lack of file-size information.

The *.*, or Star-Dot-Star, Wildcard

It is possible to specify all files with the sweeping *.* wildcard combination, often called star-dot-star. You will see examples of this later when you learn about copying, deleting, and otherwise working with groups of files. Here's an example to whet your appetite: The DOS command **COPY *.* B:** will attempt to copy all the files in the current subdirectory to a floppy disk in drive B.

You will also see star-dot-star in many Shell and Windows dialog boxes. In these instances, *.* asks the Shell or Windows to show you all files regardless of their names or extensions. You'll see examples of this later in the lesson.

The Question Mark Wildcard

The question mark wildcard can be a little confusing. A single question mark means "Show me all file names that match the rest of my criteria, and I'm willing to accept any character in place of the question mark." For instance, DIR B?B will list the file names Bob, bib, and BUB. The request DIR M? lists only files with names that are two characters long and start with the letter M.

Multiple question marks can be used together. For instance, DIR M??? will show you a list of file names that are four or fewer characters long and begin with the letter M. DIR M????? will show you file names up to six characters long beginning with M.

You can place question marks in the middle of requests (DIR M??T, for instance) or in file extensions (DIR *.T?T, perhaps).

Feel free to experiment with these, but don't let people see you or they will think you are a DOS guru. And we wouldn't want that! There are often easier ways to accomplish the same things in the Shell or Windows.

DOS Commands That Work with Wildcards

The following DOS commands will work with wildcards. You'll learn more about them later:

- DIR

- DEL

- ERASE

- COPY

- REN

Switches and Wildcards with the DOS Prompt

You can often use DOS switches and wildcards together at the DOS prompt, but it takes some patience and experimentation. For instance, if you want to see a list of all the file names on your hard disk that end in the extension TXT, you can use the DIR command with the /S switch (to search all subdirectories) and the /P switch (to pause at each screenful).

Sometimes the order of the elements of the command and the placement of spaces can be important. For instance, the command DIR/S/P*.TXT will not work, but placing a space between the P and the asterisk does the trick. Sometimes, you can rearrange the order of switches and wildcard requests. For instance, DIR *.TXT /S/P will also work.

Wildcards and the Shell

There are times when wildcards can be useful in the Shell. For example, when writing this book, I placed the hundred-plus screen illustrations in a single subdirectory called BOOKFIGS. Files were numbered with lesson and sequential figure numbers (01-01.CAP, 01-02.CAP, 02-01.CAP, and so on). It's a pretty long list of files.

To see a list of just the illustrations for Lesson 5, I can use wildcards and lesson numbers with the Shell's File Display Options command on the Shell's Options menu:

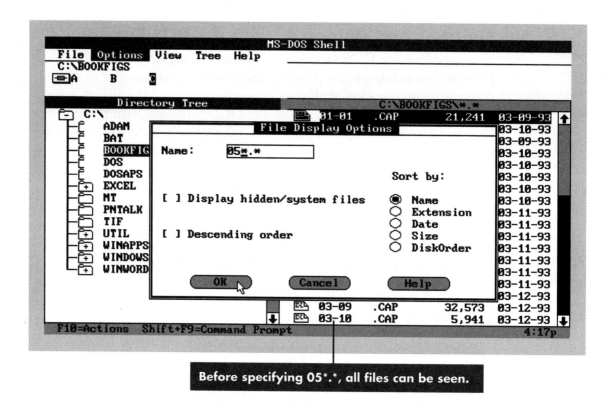

Before specifying 05*.*, all files can be seen.

In this example, I've typed **05** in front of the *.*, telling the Shell to display only file names that begin with 05. Here's the resulting display. As you can imagine, it is much easier to use since it is not cluttered with files from other lessons.

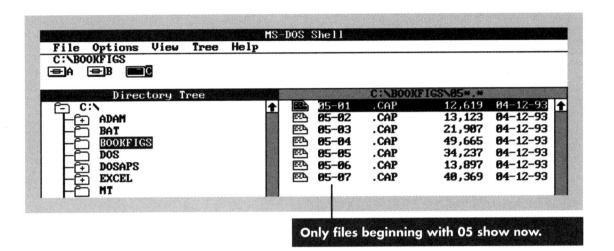

Only files beginning with 05 show now.

● **Note** Be careful when you use wildcards and text together this way. It can make you believe that you've lost files when you haven't. To see all your files, be sure you use just *.* in the Shell Name box.

The same tricks can be used in the Windows File Manager and elsewhere.

Don't Get Too Wild!

Don't get carried away with wildcards. For instance, as you will see in Lesson 9, the command DEL *.* will attempt to delete all the files in a given subdirectory. Measure twice. Cut once.

Working with Files and Directories

How do you delete old files to free up disk space? Can you recover files that you've accidentally deleted? Are there ways to improve the odds of recovery? What files should you back up and how is that done? Find out here, in Part Two.

Creating New Subdirectories

As you should know by now, disk subdirectories are places to keep related files together. Usually, when you follow the instructions that come with new programs (word processing or bookkeeping software, for instance), you create new subdirectories as part of the installation process. But most people like to create additional subdirectories to further organize things. You can use the DOS prompt, DOS Shell, or Windows to create your own subdirectories. Let's take a look.

Explore the Subdirectories You Already Have

In Lesson 4 you learned how to see lists of existing subdirectories on your disks and their contents. Every formatted disk has a root directory on it. The root directory is represented by a backslash (\). Chances are you also have a DOS subdirectory on your C: drive. If you've installed Windows, there will probably be a WINDOWS subdirectory and possibly a WINAPPS subdirectory. If you haven't done so already, take a moment to view and understand your current collection of subdirectories using the techniques described in the previous lessons.

Planning a Directory Strategy That Works for You

Before creating new subdirectories, give some thought to how you want to organize your disks. While it is possible to create subdirectories on floppies, it is not always necessary to do so. Frequently, the automatically created root directory is all that you'll need.

Creating subdirectories for files on a hard disk is often a personal thing, and the approach used will vary with the way you work. Some people need only a half-dozen subdirectories; others need hundreds. If you share a machine with others (family members, for instance), it might be useful to have a subdirectory for each user. Each person's subdirectory would contain additional subdirectories of their making.

When using networked, shared hard disks, it is very important to create workable subdirectory *strategies* that take personal, organizational, and security issues into account. It's a good idea to document shared disk organizations so that people know where to put things and where to look for them. If you work on a network, check with your network manager to learn more.

Some users create subdirectories for each application they use. For instance, they create one subdirectory for their Excel spreadsheets, another for their WordPerfect files, and so on. Others create subdirectories for each project or each client and keep a mixture of file types in these "task-specific" subdirectories (for example, client subdirectories containing combinations of spreadsheets, word processing documents, etc., for each client). Sometimes, client subdirectories are further broken down into projects or document types. For instance, law firms often establish subdirectories for clients and have "matter" or "case" and "correspondence" subdirectories within each client's subdirectories.

● Note As you will see later in this book, it's pretty easy to move things to different subdirectories, particularly if you use the Shell or Windows. So, don't worry if you fail to create the "perfect" strategy immediately.

Creating a New Subdirectory

Too much theory, let's make some subdirectories! When you name directories, you must follow the same naming rules as when you name files. Directory names can contain a maximum of eight characters and no spaces, asterisks, backslashes, and so on. You should not assign extensions to directory names.

Permissible directory names might include SALES93, 93SALES, SALES'93, and 93_SALES (note the use of the underline character instead of a space).

The following are *illegal* subdirectory names: SALES1993 (too long), SALES 93 (spaces are not permitted), SALES\93 (illegal use of a backslash—10-yard penalty), and SALES*93 (asterisks are not permitted).

Using the Shell to Create New Subdirectories

Use the Create Directory... command on the Shell's File menu to make subdirectories. With the Shell running:

1. Click on the appropriate disk icon if necessary (C:, for instance), then click on the folder representing the place where you want to create the new directory. For instance, to create a new subdirectory for the root, click on the root directory's folder, as shown here:

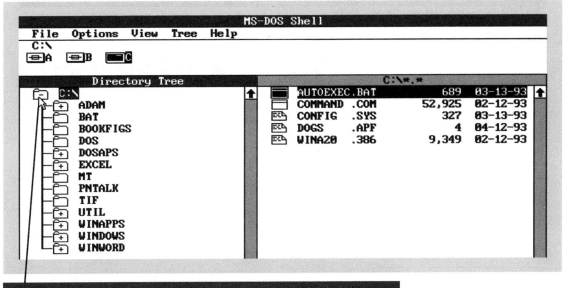

Point and click to select a "parent" for your new subdirectory.

2. Choose **Create Directory…** from the File menu:

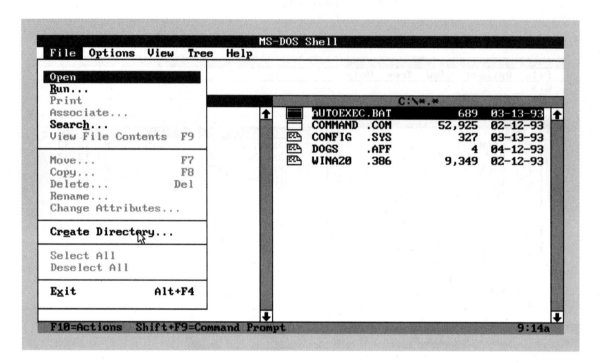

3. Type a legal subdirectory name in the dialog box (such as
sales93).

4. Click OK or press ↵ to create the subdirectory.

5. Check your work:

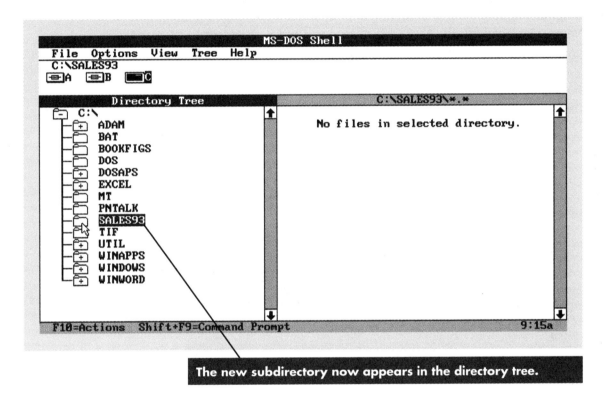

The new subdirectory now appears in the directory tree.

The Windows Method

The Windows method is nearly identical to the Shell method. Switch to the Windows File Manager, where you use the Create Directory... command on the File menu to make subdirectories.

Creating Subdirectories within Subdirectories

To place a subdirectory within another (a SMITH subdirectory within your CLIENTS subdirectory, for example), click in the Shell list to select the directory you want to use as the "parent." Once you've highlighted it, follow the steps just described.

Using the DOS MD Command to Make Subdirectories

Use the MD command (which stands for *Make Directory*) to create new subdirectories at the DOS prompt. Ironically, it can often be quicker to make new directories this way than it is to use the Shell or Windows, particularly if you are staring at the DOS prompt and don't need to place the new subdirectory several levels deep.

For instance, to create a subdirectory called SALES93 in the root directory, you would follow these steps:

1. With the root as the current directory, simply type

md\sales93

```
C:\>md\sales93
```

2. Press ↵.

That's all there is to it.

Creating subdirectories within subdirectories is only slightly harder, unless, of course, you are not a good typist or you have forgotten the exact name and order of the other subdirectories involved. For instance, to create a new LETTERS subdirectory within a SMITH subdirectory within a CLIENTS subdirectory, you would simply type

md\clients\smith\letters

```
C:\>md\clients\smith\letters
```

DOS will tell you if you've spelled existing subdirectory names wrong or have got the subdirectory "path" out of order.

Next stop: copying and moving things. You may want to take a moment to set up some new subdirectories first. You'll be organized in no time.

Copying and Moving Files and Directories

Copying or moving files and directories with the Shell or Windows can be as simple as pointing, then *dragging*. Copying or moving things at the DOS prompt—well, that can be a real *drag*.

There are lots of reasons to *copy* files. Sometimes you need the same file in more than one place on the same disk. Other times you want to copy files or directories to different disks—to hand a coworker a floppy, for instance. *Moving* is necessary when you want to reorganize a disk, or when you want to free up disk space by "archiving" old files to floppies or other disks.

While the steps for copying and moving things are quite similar, the results are obviously different. When you copy a file, you end up with two identical files in different places. When you move a file…well, you get the picture. Nearly identical, simple steps are often used for both copying and moving. Beginners and pros alike can be confused by this. Here. Let's take a look.

Make Sure You Are Ready to Copy or Move

Before copying or moving, it's a good idea to check the destination disk drive. Is there a disk in it? Is it the right type of disk (high density or low density)? Is it write-protected? (If it is, you won't be able to move or copy anything to it.)

● Note See your hardware manual for information about disk details like these. You can also check out Lesson 13 for more information on write protection and other floppy-disk issues.

Does the destination disk have enough room for the files you intend to copy? You can either add up the file sizes in your head or use the Shell's **Show Information** choice on the Options menu. Notice how it shows the combined disk space required by all three selected files:

These three files have been selected in the file-list pane.

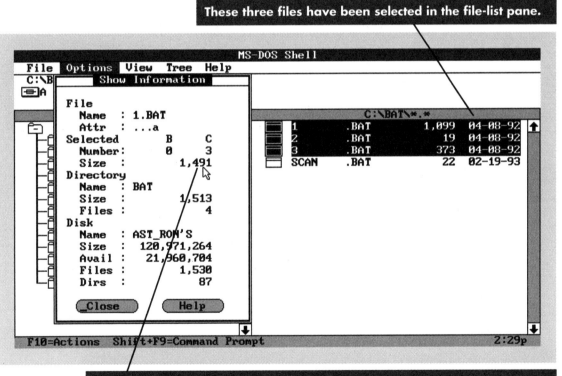

This is the space needed on the destination disk for the three selected files.

69

Copying Files to a Different Disk with the Shell

Here's an easy way to copy files to a different disk with the Shell. Select a file in the Shell's file list by pointing and clicking, then drag the resulting icon from the source drive to a *different disk's* icon (your A: or B: drive, perhaps). For instance, to copy a file from your C: drive to a floppy in the B: drive:

1. With the Shell running and with a disk in the B: drive, point to the file on your C: drive that you wish to copy (you can point to the icon or any part of the name).

2. Hold down the mouse button and start to drag. The pointer will change to the plus icon. Drag the icon until it is directly over the destination disk's drive icon. The letter next to the disk's icon will be highlighted when you've reached the sweet spot (the B: drive in this example). Release the mouse button when you get there.

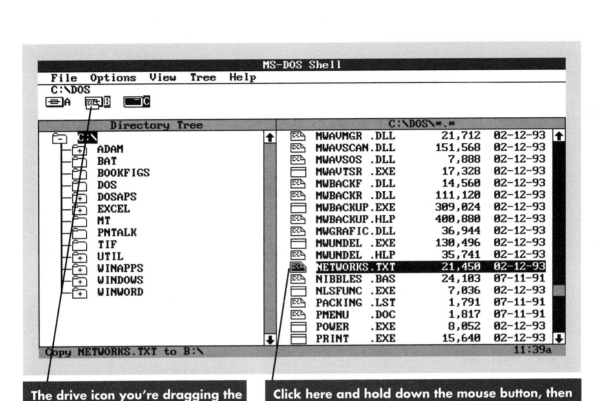

The drive icon you're dragging the NETWORKS.TXT file to

Click here and hold down the mouse button, then drag to a different drive's icon.

3. If all goes well, you'll be asked to confirm the copy request. Click Yes or tap ↵:

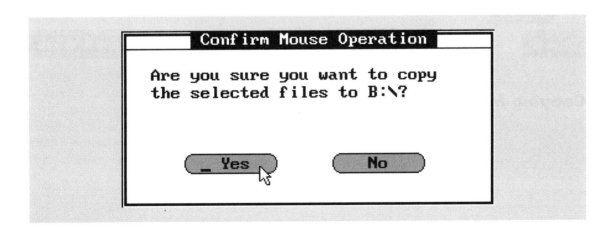

Shortly after you confirm the copy request, you should be able to see
two copies of the file—one on the source disk and one on the destination disk. In this illustration the **Dual File Lists** choice on the Shell's
View menu was used to display the contents of both the C: and B:
drives:

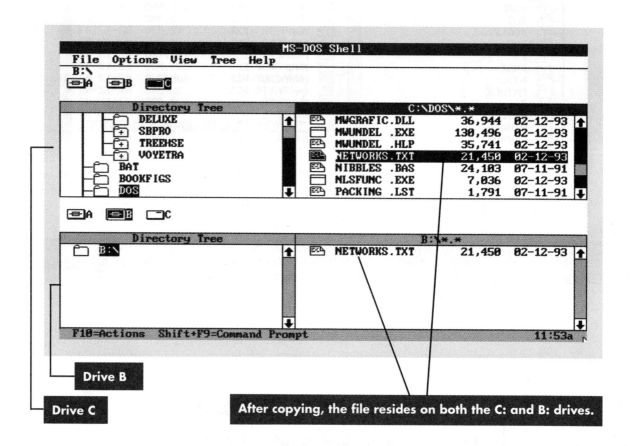

Copying Multiple Files Simultaneously

You can select multiple files in the Shell's file list before dragging, then
copy them all at once. Do this by using Shift-clicking and the other selection techniques you learned in earlier lessons. Then, when you drag,

all the selected files will follow. Notice the slight difference in the appearance of the mouse pointer when dragging multiple files:

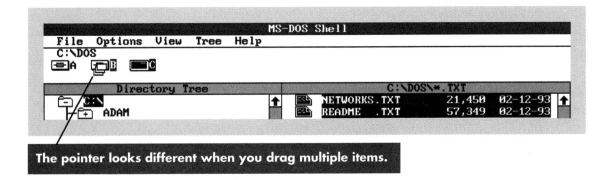

The pointer looks different when you drag multiple items.

Using Windows to Copy Files to Different Disks

The Windows File Manager works files almost exactly like the Shell where file copying to different disks is concerned.

Copying Files to Different Subdirectories on the Same Disk

When using the Shell (or Windows) to copy files to different subdirectories on the same disk, hold down the Ctrl key when you drag. You will be asked to confirm the copy request. If you forget to hold down the Ctrl key when you drag, you'll be asked to confirm a *move* request. Click No and try again.

● Note You may need to scroll to see the folder for the destination subdirectory, or even open a second window (using the Dual File Lists option) to display your destination folder. Use the tricks you learned in Lesson 4 to do this.

Copying Files with the DOS COPY Command

Copying files with the DOS COPY command requires attention to detail and at least one *skilled* typing finger. And, you need to remember the exact name and extension of the file being copied. It's not all that quick or easy. That's why so many people prefer the Shell or Windows.

In some situations—using the COPY command to copy a file from the root directory of one disk to the root of another, for instance—you *can* leave out some of the detail if you know what you are doing. And you can use wildcards to copy multiple files at once if they have similar names. But in general, DOS needs to be told

- The source drive's name (C:, for instance)

- The subdirectory's name (BATCH, for instance)

- The destination drive's name (B:, perhaps)

- The destination subdirectory

- The name of the file or files being copied (1.BAT or *.BAT, for instance)

Suppose you want to copy your AUTOEXEC.BAT file from your C: drive to a floppy in the A: drive. Here's one way to do that with the COPY command:

1. Make sure the destination disk is ready and has sufficient free space for the file being copied (A: in this example).

2. Type **COPY** and a space.

3. Type the path and file name of the source file (**C:\AUTO-EXEC.BAT** in this example).

4. Type another space.

5. Type the destination drive name (**A:**, for instance) and an optional path if you want the file to be copied into other than the root directory of the destination drive. Your screen might look something like this:

```
C:\>copy c:\autoexec.bat a:
```

There are lots of shortcuts and tricks you can use with the DOS COPY command. For instance, in the previous example, I could have left out the C:\ portion of the command, since I was already "logged on" to the C: drive's root directory. But details like that are beyond the scope of this book. You can read about them in DOS 6's online help, or see the Appendix at the back of this book for suggested fountains of wisdom.

Moving Files with the Shell or Windows

There are many ways to move files with the Shell or the Windows File Manager. I think the easiest is to simply drag them from one directory to another with your mouse. Here's an example of that in the Shell:

1. Locate the file to be moved—in this case, **07-07.CAP** in C:\, the root directory.

2. Drag it to the folder for the sudirectory where you want to move the file—in this case, **BOOKFIGS**. The folder's name will be highlighted when you've reached the right spot.

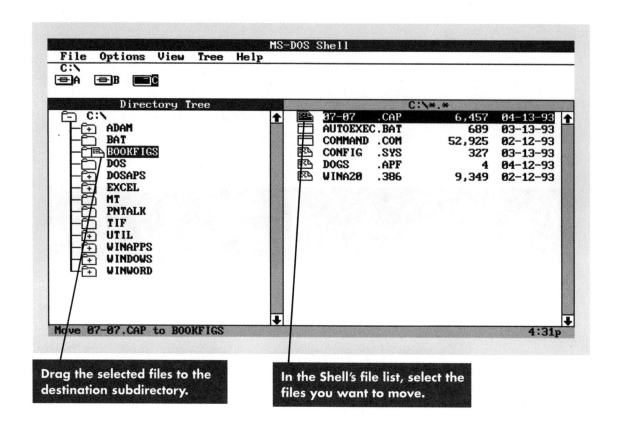

Drag the selected files to the destination subdirectory.

In the Shell's file list, select the files you want to move.

3. Release the mouse button. You'll see a dialog box pop up, asking you if this is something you really want to do. Confirm the move by clicking the Yes button or tapping the ↵ key.

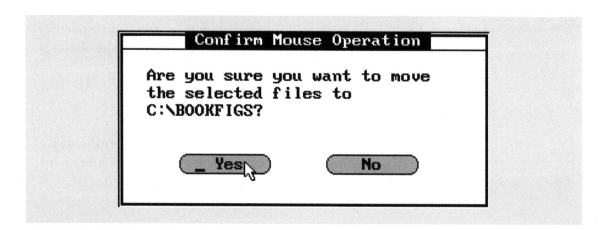

The same techniques work in Windows' File Manager. Since both Windows and the Shell let you display multiple drives (or different views of the same drive) simultaneously, you can easily move things from one disk to another or from one directory to another.

So how come dragging *copies* sometimes and *moves* other times?

Got me. Someone at Microsoft decided that this makes sense, so it does. Think of it this way: When you drag things around on the *same disk,* you *move* them from place to place. When you drag them from *one disk to another,* you *copy* them. Using the Ctrl key when you drag always copies, so while it is not necessary to do so, hold it down whenever you want to copy, if that helps make things less confusing (Ctrl-mouse for Copy, Mouse for Move).

Moving Files to a Different Disk

You *can* use the mouse to move files to a different disk. Hold down the Alt key while you drag the selected files to the destination drive.

Moving Files with the DOS MOVE Command

The brand-new, long-awaited MOVE command in DOS 6 is every bit as ugly as the old COPY command. The safest way to ensure perfection is to include drive letters and paths in your command. For instance, to use the MOVE command to move the file shown in the previous example, you type

```
MOVE C:\07.06-CAP C:\BOOKFIGS
```

Stick with the Shell or File Manager if you can. It's nice to have the confirmation dialog box, so you don't accidentally move something you didn't intend to, and there's less typing.

Moving Subdirectories and Their Contents

If you have Windows, the easiest way to move a subdirectory and its files is to drag the subdirectory's icon in the File Manager. You can move subdirectories with the DOS Shell, but it's a pain. Using the DOS command to move entire subdirectories is bloodier still. So let's look at the easy way first:

1. With the Windows File Manager active, select the subdirectory you wish to move by clicking on its corresponding folder.

2. Drag the folder to the new location (a different subdirectory, for instance).

3. Confirm the move by clicking OK or pressing ↵.

4. Check to see that the results are what you expected.

Moving Subdirectories with the Shell and DOS Commands

To move subdirectories and their contents, you don't actually relocate them. Instead, you

1. Set up new subdirectories where you want them.

2. Copy the old files into the new directories.

3. Delete the old files and directories.

Yuck. Use *Windows* for moving directories and their contents. If you must use the Shell or DOS, you'll need to know how to delete files and directories, a topic covered in Lesson 9. But first (as they say on television), let's look at *renaming* things in the next lesson.

Renaming Files and Directories

Macintosh users will smirk when they read this lesson (that is unless someone took away their Macs). Renaming files and directories in the DOS world is—well, it's more work than it should be. As usual, the Shell may be the easiest place to rename things, so let's start there. First, a reminder and an important warning.

File and Subdirectory Naming Rules

Although you've read most of this in earlier lessons, it's worth repeating the essentials of file and subdirectory naming Zen here:

- Maximum of eight characters plus an optional three-character extension (12345678.123).

- DOS treats upper- and lowercase letters as the same things.

- No "reserved" characters allowed (\, *, ?, etc.).

- No spaces in names (use the underline character, _, instead).

- Extensions are not recommended when naming directories.

- No identical file names in the same subdirectory.

- No identical subdirectory names in the same parent directory (you can't have two subdirectories called BATCH in the root, for instance).

- No shouting or running in the halls.

Read This or Weep!

Just because it's *your* personal computer doesn't mean you can do any darn thing you want with it! Bespectacled computer scientists and engineers have spent years making your computer nearly impossible to understand. It's a wonder the things work at all. Your computer "expects" to find certain files with precise file names in very specific places.

For instance, if you decide to change the name of that funky old COMMAND.COM file in your root directory, or move it to a different directory, your pride and joy won't work the next time you switch it on. Or, if you change the name of an important subdirectory, programs that use the subdirectory may not be able to find their files.

Things might not work right when you start the computer, or they may work fine until you try to run a particular program or perform a specific task, like spell-checking a word processing document. You might even see messages claiming that your important files don't exist, even when they are all just fine. Consultants make a fine living undoing people's clever renaming and reorganizing schemes. So before you give random files or subdirectories the names of the seven dwarfs, be sure you understand the consequences.

Stick to renaming just document files you've created and subdirectories that you've set up on your own. Leave the *files* in the root directory (usually C:\) alone! Don't mess with things in the DOS subdirectory either. In general, if you don't know what a file or subdirectory does—or who put it there—find out before changing or deleting it. There. I've warned you.

Renaming Files with the Shell

OK. Fire up the Shell, if you like, or just read along and look at the pictures.

To rename one or more files with the Shell:

1. Start by selecting the file or files you want to rename. Notice the selected file here. It's the file for one of the illustrations from this book, and it's missing a file extension:

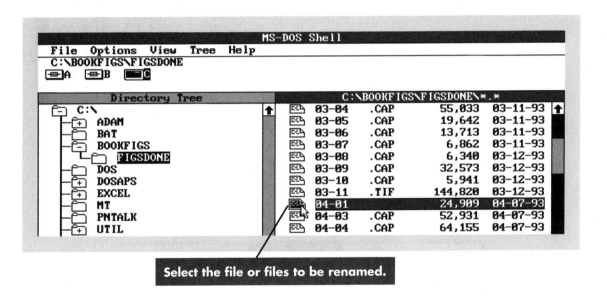

Select the file or files to be renamed.

2. Choose Rename... from the File menu.

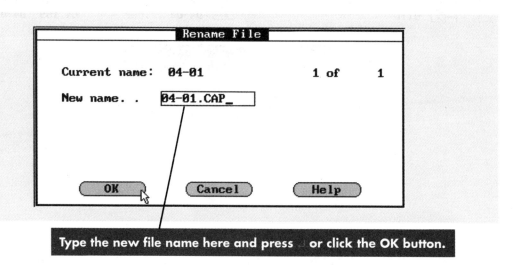

```
                          MS-DOS Shell
 File  Options  View  Tree  Help

   Open
   Run...
   Print                                    C:\BOOKFIGS\FIGSDONE\*.*
   Associate...                   ↑    📁  03-04   .CAP      55,033   03-11-93  ↑
   Search...                           📁  03-05   .CAP      19,642   03-11-93
   View File Contents    F9            📁  03-06   .CAP      13,713   03-11-93
                                       📁  03-07   .CAP       6,862   03-11-93
   Move...               F7            📁  03-08   .CAP       6,340   03-12-93
   Copy...               F8            📁  03-09   .CAP      32,573   03-12-93
   Delete...             Del           📁  03-10   .CAP       5,941   03-12-93
   Rename...                           📁  03-11   .TIF     144,820   03-12-93
   Change Attributes...⤸               📁  04-01              24,909   04-07-93
                                       📁  04-03   .CAP      52,931   04-07-93
   Create Directory...                 📁  04-04   .CAP      64,155   04-07-93
                                       📁  04-05   .CAP      59,270   04-07-93
   Select All                          📁  04-06   .CAP      59,108   04-10-93
   Deselect All                        📁  04-07   .CAP      52,809   04-07-93
                                       📁  04-08   .CAP      65,076   04-07-93
   Exit                  Alt+F4        📁  04-09   .CAP      47,593   04-07-93
                                       📁  04-10   .CAP       6,088   04-10-93
                                   ↓   📁  04-11   .CAP      28,645   04-10-93  ↓
 F10=Actions  Shift+F9=Command Prompt                              10:36a
```

3. Type a new name in the Rename File dialog box.

```
 ┌──────────────── Rename File ────────────────┐
 │                                              │
 │   Current name:  04-01            1 of    1  │
 │                                              │
 │   New name. .  ┌─────────────┐               │
 │                │04-01.CAP_    │               │
 │                └─────────────┘               │
 │                                              │
 │                                              │
 │     ( OK )      ( Cancel )      ( Help )      │
 │         ⤸                                    │
 └──────────────────────────────────────────────┘
```

Type the new file name here and press ↵ or click the OK button.

4. Click OK or press ↵ to make the change.

5. If you've selected more than one file to rename, you'll be prompted for the remaining files one at a time.

Renaming Subdirectories with the Shell

Renaming subdirectories is nearly identical to renaming files when you're using the Shell.

1. Start by selecting the subdirectory or subdirectories you want to rename.

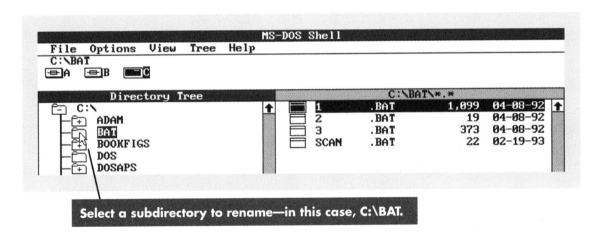

Select a subdirectory to rename—in this case, **C:\BAT.**

2. Choose Rename... from the File menu just as before.

3. Type a new name in the Rename Directory dialog box.

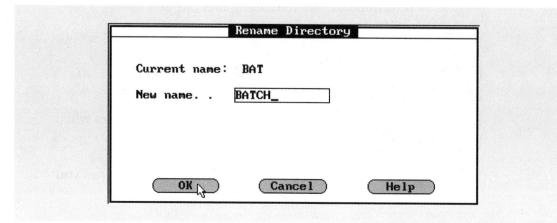

4. Click OK or press ↵ to make the change.

5. If you've selected more than one subdirectory to rename,
you'll be prompted for the remaining changes one at a time.

● **Note** If the directory change affects the path in your AUTOEXEC.BAT
file (see Lesson 18), update the path.

Renaming Files and Subdirectories with Windows

Use the Windows File Manager to change file or subdirectory names.
The steps for renaming a single file or subdirectory are almost identical
to the Shell method—use the Rename... command on the File menu.

Renaming Files from the DOS Prompt

To rename a file from the DOS prompt, use the DOS REN command.
It requires the old file name, the new file name, and path information
if you are not in the subdirectory containing the file.

For instance, suppose you are in the root directory and decide to re-name the 04-01 illustration file used in the earlier examples:

1. Type REN and a space.

2. Type the path to the old file name, if necessary (C:\BOOK-FIGS\FIGSDONE\04-01 in our example).

3. Type a space.

4. Type the new file name (04-01.CAP in our example).

```
C:\>REN C:\BOOKFIGS\FIGSDONE\04-01 04-01.CAP
```

5. Press ↵ to execute the command.

 Note Wildcards work here. For instance, to rename all the extensions in our example from .CAP to .TIF, you could use the command REN C:\BOOKFIGS\FIGSDONE*.CAP *.TIF. Use care, though.

Renaming Subdirectories from the DOS Prompt

It seems logical that some version of the DOS rename command would rename directories too, right? Wrong! Use the DOS MOVE command instead.

Suppose you want to rename the BAT subdirectory BATCH. While in the root directory:

1. Type MOVE.

2. Type a space.

3. Type the old subdirectory name (**BAT**).

4. Type another space.

5. Type the new subdirectory name (**BATCH**).

6. Press ↵.

7. DOS will confirm the renaming with the cryptic response shown at the bottom of this illustration:

```
C:\>DIR *.

 Volume in drive C is AST_RON'S
 Volume Serial Number is 1A57-78F1
 Directory of C:\

BAT          <DIR>      03-09-93    6:30p
DOS          <DIR>      01-08-92   10:35a
ADAM         <DIR>      03-09-93    6:36p
UTIL         <DIR>      01-08-92   10:36a
WINDOWS      <DIR>      01-08-92   10:36a
WINAPPS      <DIR>      01-08-92   10:38a
DOSAPS       <DIR>      03-10-93    9:25a
MT           <DIR>      04-07-93    2:36p
BOOKFIGS     <DIR>      03-12-93    9:21a
EXCEL        <DIR>      03-12-93   10:18a
PNTALK       <DIR>      03-18-92    4:43p
WINWORD      <DIR>      03-12-93   10:19a
        12 file(s)             0 bytes
                       21327872 bytes free

C:\>MOVE BAT BATCH
c:\bat => c:\batch [ok]

C:\>
```

Type this.

DOS confirms the name change.

**This directory listing shows that the
old subdirectory name was BAT.**

Checking the directory list again shows that the change has been made:

```
C:\>DIR *.

 Volume in drive C is AST_RON'S
 Volume Serial Number is 1A57-78F1
 Directory of C:\

BATCH          <DIR>      03-09-93    6:30p
DOS            <DIR>      01-08-92   10:35a
ADAM           <DIR>      03-09-93    6:36p
UTIL           <DIR>      01-08-92   10:36a
WINDOWS        <DIR>      01-08-92   10:36a
```

The subdirectory name has been changed.

When necessary, you'll need to include the path to the old directory name in step 3.

Next stop—deleting things.

15 MINUTES

Deleting Files and Directories

Do you have newspapers on your credenza from ten years ago? Or are you like me, a person who throws out his lunch before he's eaten it? Either way, eventually, you'll need to know how to get rid of unwanted files and directories on your disk. And you've come to the right place.

Before you start trashing, however, consider "archiving" some of those old files to floppies or some other storage media. You'd be amazed at how often you'll wish you could go back to some old version of a document, or reuse part of a spreadsheet from a year or two ago. When in doubt, save a copy to a floppy before deleting useful things from a hard disk.

One more caution before we continue. DOS, Windows, and particularly the Shell can make it brutally easy for you to inadvertently delete things. If you notice an accidental deletion soon enough, you *might* be able to recover the deleted item. But this is not always the case. Work carefully. Turn on all the available "lifesaving" features, like deletion confirmations (described in this lesson) and Delete Sentry (described in Lesson 10). In fact, if you are a new computer user, or you are worried about the contents of your hard disk, you may want to read Lesson 10 after you read this lesson but before you try the techniques described here.

Deleting Files with the Shell

Deleting files with the Shell can literally be *too* easy. It can be as simple as selecting a file in the file list and tapping the Delete key once. Poof. Gone. History. Not even a noise.

If you *hold down* the Delete key for a while, additional files will be squirted like watermelon seeds out of the universe, one after the next. If you have a cat at home, and if it steps on your Delete key, you could be outa business. Unless, of course, you've enabled the Shell's Confirm on Delete feature. So let's make sure yours is turned on:

1. With the Shell running, choose **Confirmation…** from its Options menu. You'll see a dialog box like this one:

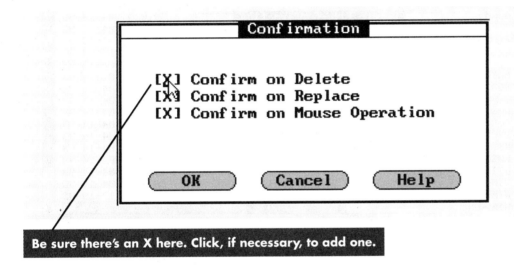

Be sure there's an X here. Click, if necessary, to add one.

2. Be sure there are X's in *all three* boxes, particularly the one labeled **Confirm on Delete**. Point and click where the X belongs to add one, if necessary.

3. Click OK or press ↵.

You only need to change this setting once. Henceforth, you'll be visited by a cursed confirmation box each time you attempt to delete something.

Deleting a Single File with the Shell

1. Click on a file in the Shell's file list to select (highlight) it—in this example, LOGO.TIF.

2. Press the Delete key or use the File menu's Delete... option. The Shell will ask if that's what you really want to do:

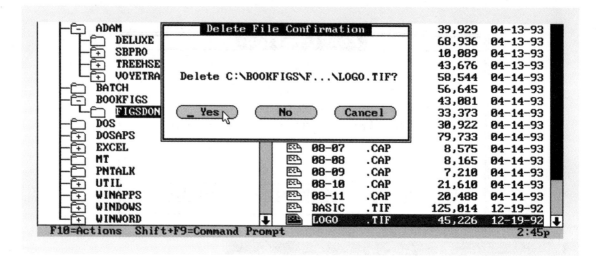

```
┌─ADAM                    Delete File Confirmation        39,929  04-13-93
│  └─ DELUXE                                              68,936  04-13-93
│     ┌─ SBPRO                                            10,089  04-13-93
│     ┌─ TREEHSE                                          43,676  04-13-93
│     ┌─ VOYETRA    Delete C:\BOOKFIGS\F...\LOGO.TIF?     58,544  04-14-93
│  BATCH                                                  56,645  04-14-93
└─ BOOKFIGS                                               43,081  04-14-93
   └─ FIGSDON      ( _ Yes )    ( No )    ( Cancel )      33,373  04-14-93
   DOS                                                    30,922  04-14-93
   DOSAPS                                                 79,733  04-14-93
   EXCEL                        08-07    .CAP             8,575   04-14-93
   MT                           08-08    .CAP             8,165   04-14-93
   PNTALK                       08-09    .CAP             7,210   04-14-93
   UTIL                         08-10    .CAP             21,610  04-14-93
   WINAPPS                      08-11    .CAP             20,488  04-14-93
   WINDOWS                      BASIC    .TIF             125,014 12-19-92
   WINWORD                      LOGO     .TIF             45,226  12-19-92
F10=Actions  Shift+F9=Command Prompt                              2:45p
```

3. Click Yes to confirm the deletion. Poof.

• Note Instead of clicking the Yes button with the mouse, you can just tap the ↵ key to confirm deletions. This is a two-edged sword. It makes things quicker, but it is very, *very* easy to get in the habit of tapping that ↵ key without looking at your screen, which defeats the purpose of the confirmation step. It's your call. I say, get in the habit of looking, pointing, and clicking—at least till you become a DOS wonk.

Deleting Multiple Files with the Shell

If you know how to select multiple files in the Shell's file list, you know
how to delete them:

1. Point and click to select the first file you wish to delete.

2. Shift-click to select a continuous range of files, or hold
down the Ctrl key while you point to files scattered throughout the list.

3. When you've selected all your victims, press the Delete key
or use the File menu's Delete... option. You'll see a confirmation dialog box with a partial list of the all the files to be
deleted:

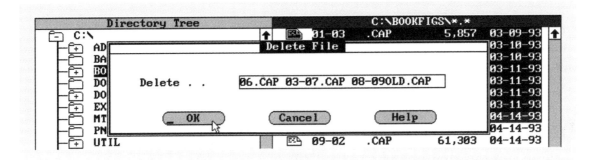

4. Click OK to start the process. You'll be prompted before
each separate deletion (a sort of "Are you really, *really* sure?").

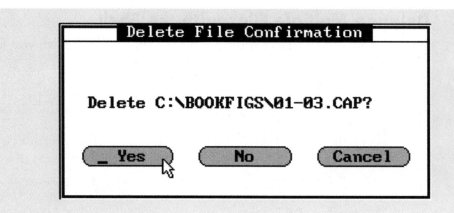

5. Click Yes each time to delete a file or click No to spare the current file from deletion and move on to the next. Choosing Cancel aborts the deletion process, but it won't bring back files already deleted.

Incidentally, Windows has a slightly more convenient way to delete multiple files, so if you do this often, and if you use Windows, check out the File Manager's deletion features.

Deleting Files at the DOS Prompt

A glutton for punishment, huh? Yes, in DOS 6 you can delete things at the DOS prompt by typing either the command DEL or ERASE (they do the same thing), followed by the complete file name, including its extension if any. When you are not currently "logged in" to the subdirectory containing the file, you'll need to include the path.

For example, if you are in the root directory and want to delete a file called LOGO.TIF in the subdirectory FIGSDONE (a subdirectory of BOOKFIGS), you would

1. Type the command DEL (or ERASE) and a space.

2. Type the path to the file (C:\BOOKFIGS\FIGSDONE\).

3. Type the file name, including its extension (**LOGO.TIF**).

```
C:\>del c:\bookfigs\figsdone\logo.tif
```

4. Press ↵.

Except for a soft whir, you'll see or hear nothing unusual, but the file will be gone. A pretty unsatisfying lot of typing, if you ask me.

● Note If you see the message "Bad command or file name," DOS is telling you that it is as confused as you are. You've typed the wrong command (DELETE, for instance), or the wrong file name, or an incorrect path, or no path at all. Check your work. Since computers never make mistakes, it must be something *you've* done. Yeah, right.

By the way, wonk wannabees, wildcards work here too. The command

DEL B:*.*

will attempt to erase everything on that floppy in your B: drive. Are you sure that's what you want to do?

Or you can use wildcards to delete multiple files with things in common. For instance, here's how to delete all the files with the extension TMP in the root directory:

```
C:\>del *.tmp
```

Deleting Subdirectories

That's it. You've had it with that (bleeping) client and you want to be rid of every trace: All the files and the subdirectories containing them. Deleting subdirectories and their contents may actually be easiest at the DOS prompt. But since this can be such a destructive process, let's look at the wimp's (err, I mean the "graphical user's") way first—using the Shell.

Deleting Subdirectories with the Shell

Before you can delete a subdirectory with the Shell, you must first delete all the files (and other subdirectories) contained with in it. Ugh.

Suppose, for example you have a subdirectory called STOOGES, and it contains three files. Start by using the Shell to delete the files:

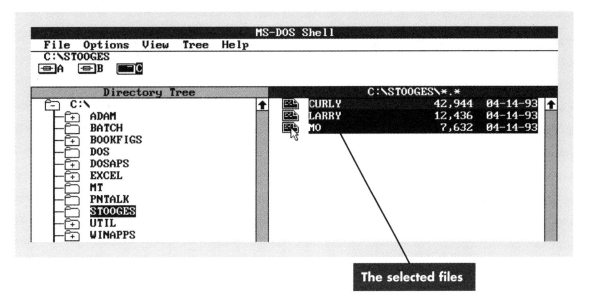

The selected files

1. Shift-select all the files in the list:

2. Press the Delete key to start the deletion process.

3. Confirm the deletions (you do have confirmation turned on, don't you?).

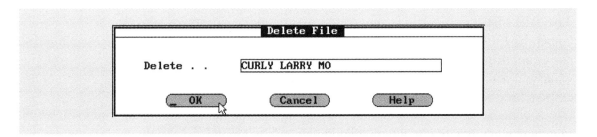

4. With the files gone, highlight the folder representing the subdirectory you wish to delete by clicking on it (**STOOGES** in this example).

5. Press the Delete key or use the Delete choice from the File menu. You'll get the delete confirmation box.

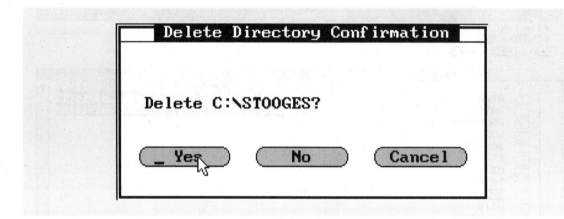

6. Confirm the directory deletion by choosing Yes.

Deleting Subdirectories with Windows

Deleting subdirectories with the Windows File Manager is similar to the Shell method, but you need not delete the files first. You can have Windows prompt you before it deletes each file or subdirectory, or you can have Windows wipe out everything in one fell swoop.

Deleting Subdirectories at the DOS Prompt

The DELTREE command is one of the reasons power users love DOS 6 and the DOS prompt. This simple command can obliterate just about anything (and everything) you own. DOS will even ask if that's what you really want to do, then tell you that it is doing it! (DOS has come a long way over the years!).

For example, while in the root directory, to kill off CURLY, LARRY, MO, and the subdirectory that holds them, simply follow these steps:

1. Type DELTREE and a space.

2. Type the subdirectory name and a path, if necessary (STOOGES in our example).

3. Press ↵. DOS will ask you to confirm the deletion.

4. Type Y and press ↵ (or N and ↵ to abort).

DOS will make your computer whir and buzz…and the deed will be done.

```
C:\>deltree stooges
Delete directory "stooges" and all its subdirectories? [yn] y
Deleting stooges...

C:\>
```

Alas, poor Mo.

Next on the agenda—getting back things you've accidentally deleted.

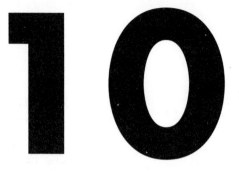

Recovering Accidentally Deleted Files

I lied earlier. Files aren't actually "squirted out of the universe" when you delete them. They flow through your computer's AC cord, back to the power company (unless, of course, you are using a battery-powered laptop).

Seriously, when you delete or erase files, they don't disappear from your disk immediately. The DEL and ERASE commands, or their Shell equivalents, simply tell DOS that the disk space occupied by the unwanted files is available for reuse. In effect, DOS "forgets" the location of the deleted files, thereby freeing the disk space. The next time DOS writes to the disk it may or may not clobber the "deleted" files.

If you are lucky (very, *very* lucky), and if you catch your deletions in time, you can often recover files or even entire directories. Moreover, there are some things you can do to improve your odds.

DOS 6 provides two UNDELETE commands—one for use at the DOS prompt and another for use from within Windows. Microsoft claims that sometimes the DOS prompt method can undelete things that the Windows version can't, but since that's not been my experience, and since the Windows version makes it easier to see what's going on, let's start with mouse in hand. But first, a word about levels of deletion protection.

Levels of Deletion Protection

DOS 6 offers three levels of deletion protection, with some interesting trade-offs. The levels are

- Standard Protection (the poorest, and automatic, choice)

- Delete Sentry (the best, but disk and RAM hungry, choice)

- Delete Tracker (the Olds Cutlass of choices)

Standard Protection (also called MS-DOS Protection in DOS 6's on-line help and elsewhere) is extremely unreliable and, I think, as good as nothing at all. That's what you get automatically when you install DOS. You need to change it. But to what?

Delete Sentry offers the best chance of success but robs you of some available RAM and much of your disk space. However, unless you have a very full hard disk and are always having insufficient RAM problems, I vote for this option.

The Delete Tracker option falls somewhere in between. Not fancy but better than a sharp stick in the eye.

Setting Protection Options via Windows

You start the Windows Undelete program from the Windows Program Manager. Double-click on the Undelete icon in the Microsoft Tools group:

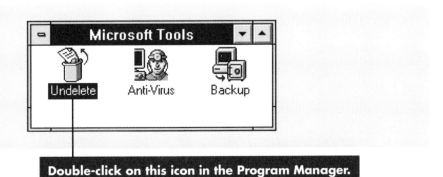

Double-click on this icon in the Program Manager.

The very first thing you'll probably want to do is enable Delete Sentry:

1. Choose Configure Delete Protection from the Options menu.

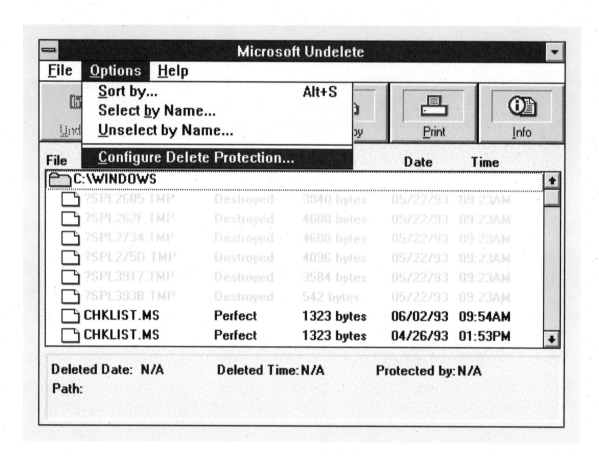

2. Click on Delete Sentry.

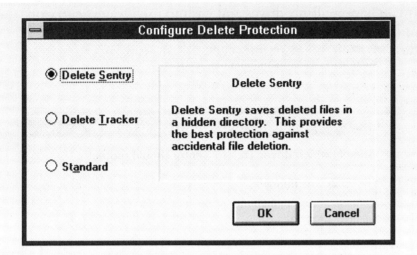

3. Choose All files here, or stick with the default options to keep things simple. In either case, click OK.

4. If you have multiple drives and wish to use Delete Sentry on only one of them, click the **Drives** button to see this window (to keep things simple, click OK instead):

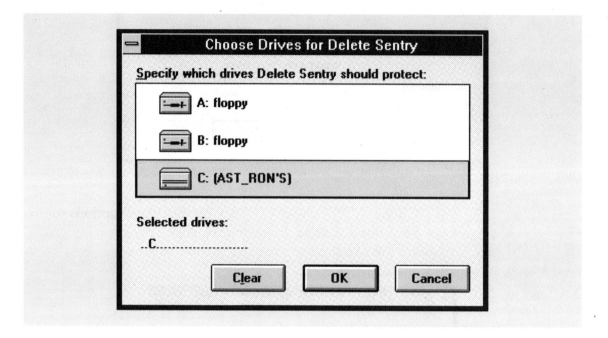

5. Pick the drive or drives you wish to protect, then click OK.

6. Windows will ask you if you want to update your AUTO-EXEC.BAT file, a necessary next step. Click OK to authorize the changes.

7. Although this doesn't always happen properly, you *should* be prompted to press Ctrl-Alt-Del to reboot your computer. (Get a guru to help you if you try steps 1 through 5 more than twice without being asked about updating your AUTOEXEC.BAT file.)

8. When you do get prompted to reboot with the Ctrl-Alt-Del key combination, *quit Windows first,* even though that's not mentioned on-screen!

9. Reboot your computer, and watch the nonsense fly by as your AUTOEXEC.BAT file sets up your computer. You should see something about Delete Sentry being enabled for one or more of your drives. If not, get thee to a DOS wonk!

Undeleting with Windows

If you haven't lost your mind from the installation process, you might
want to try to undelete some *unimportant* things before you need to
work with the real things. The best way is to use File Manager to make
some copies of several actual files in a different subdirectory from the
originals, then delete the copies (not the originals) and see if you can
undelete them.

Here are the general steps for undeleting from Windows:

1. Start the Undelete program by clicking on its icon in the
   Program Manager's Microsoft Tools window (shown in this
   lesson's first illustration).

You'll see a list of recently deleted files and subdirectories. Don't panic
when you don't see the files you want to undelete. You are looking at
files that have been deleted from your Windows subdirectory.

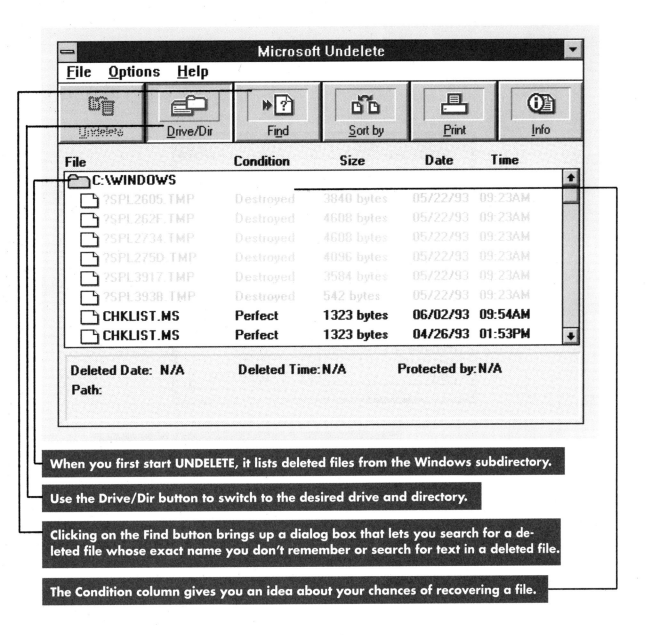

When you first start UNDELETE, it lists deleted files from the Windows subdirectory.

Use the Drive/Dir button to switch to the desired drive and directory.

Clicking on the Find button brings up a dialog box that lets you search for a deleted file whose exact name you don't remember or search for text in a deleted file.

The Condition column gives you an idea about your chances of recovering a file.

2. Click on the Drive/Dir button to see a list of available drives and subdirectories.

3. Point and click to pick the drive and then the subdirectory of interest (C:\TRAVEL in this example). Then click OK.

```
┌─────────────────────────────────────────────┐
│ ▬    Change Drive and Directory              │
│                                              │
│ Change to Directory:                         │
│ ┌──────────────────────────────────────────┐│
│ │travel\                                     ││
│ └──────────────────────────────────────────┘│
│                                              │
│ Directory:   c:\                             │
│                                              │
│ Directories:                                 │
│ ┌──────────────────┐ ▲   ┌──────────────┐   │
│ │[pntalk]          │ █   │     OK       │   │
│ │[snappro]         │ █   └──────────────┘   │
│ │[travel]          │ █                      │
│ │[util]            │ █   ┌──────────────┐   │
│ │[winapps]         │ █   │   Cancel     │   │
│ │[windows]         │ █   └──────────────┘   │
│ │[winword]         │ █                      │
│ │[-a-]             │ ▼   ┌──────────────┐   │
│ └──────────────────┘     │  Directory   │   │
│                          └──────────────┘   │
└─────────────────────────────────────────────┘
```

Use this list to pick a drive, then a subdirectory.

Shortly after you click OK in the Change Drive and Directory dialog box, you should see a list of recently deleted files, including your practice ones. Take a look at this example:

Click to undelete selected files.

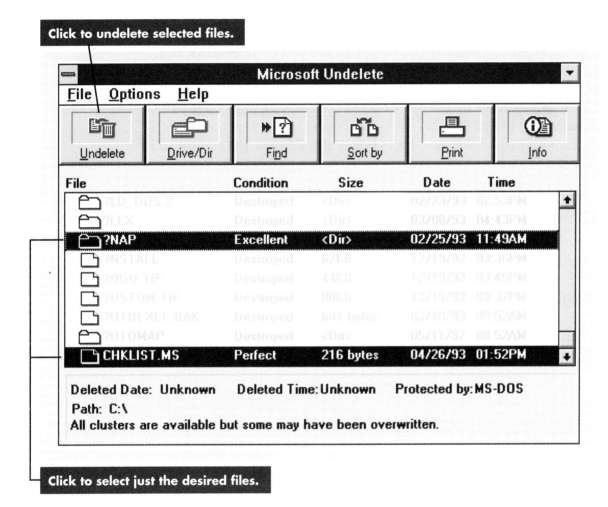

File	Condition	Size	Date	Time
?LD_DOS.2	Destroyed	<Dir>	02/23/93	02:53PM
?LEX	Destroyed	<Dir>	03/08/93	04:43PM
?NAP	Excellent	<Dir>	02/25/93	11:49AM
?NSTALL	Destroyed	62KB	12/19/92	03:36PM
?OGO.TIF	Destroyed	44KB	12/19/92	03:45PM
?USTOM.TIF	Destroyed	80KB	12/19/92	03:37PM
?UTOEXEC.BAK	Destroyed	681 bytes	03/10/93	09:52AM
?UTOMAP	Destroyed	<Dir>	05/11/92	08:52AM
CHKLIST.MS	Perfect	216 bytes	04/26/93	01:52PM

Deleted Date: Unknown   Deleted Time: Unknown   Protected by: MS-DOS
Path: C:\
All clusters are available but some may have been overwritten.

Click to select just the desired files.

4. Click on each file that you wish to restore. Clicking a second time on a selected file name will deselect it. In this example ?NAP/ and CHKLIST.MS are selected. Dimmed files cannot be recovered, at least not by Windows Undelete.

5. With recoverable files selected, click the **Undelete** button and see what happens. With any luck, you'll be pleasantly surprised.

The DOS Prompt's UNDELETE Command

The DOS prompt version of UNDELETE is not quite as quick and easy as the Windows version, but it is worth knowing about. We'll look at a few of the more common techniques. There are far too many variations and switches to describe in detail here, but they are fairly well documented in online help (type HELP UNDELETE at the DOS prompt for help). The "big" DOS books also describe the command in detail.

Things to Think about First

If you plan to use the DOS prompt version of UNDELETE with the recommended Delete Sentry (see "Levels of Deletion Protection" earlier in this lesson), you either need to type a specific DOS command *each time* you start your computer or need to modify your AUTO-EXEC.BAT file so that it does the job for you. In the simplest case, the command that you need to type (or include in your AUTOEXEC.BAT file) is

UNDELETE /S

This sets up a Delete Sentry for your boot drive (typically C:). If you have a more complex setup, check the online help screens or a bigger book.

● Note See Lesson 18 to learn how to change your AUTOEXEC.BAT file.

Undeleting at the DOS Prompt
Simply type

UNDELETE

and optionally a path to the deleted files. For instance, while in the root directory, typing UNDELETE will give you an opportunity to review and potentially recover deleted files in the root directory. Here's an example of that:

The command

```
C:\>UNDELETE

UNDELETE - A delete protection facility
Copyright (C) 1987-1993 Central Point Software, Inc.
All rights reserved.

Directory: C:\
File Specifications: *.*

    Delete Sentry control file contains    1 deleted files.

    Deletion-tracking file not found.

    MS-DOS directory contains   26 deleted files.
    Of those,    2 files may be recovered.

Using the Delete Sentry method.

    ~$TOEXEC BAT      51  4-16-93 12:32p  H..A  Deleted:  4-16-93 12:32p
This file can be 100% undeleted. Undelete (Y/N)?
```

The response

Type Y to recover the file.

Including a path in your UNDELETE command will let you examine a specific subdirectory. For instance, UNDELETE \DOS would inspect the DOS subdirectory on your current drive, while UNDELETE B:\ would inspect the root directory on a disk in drive B.

When more than one method of recovery is possible (Delete Sentry and Delete Tracker, for instance), you can force DOS to use one or another by adding switches at the DOS prompt. For instance, UNDELETE /DT recovers only files listed in the deletion-tracking file—but we're getting unquick and uneasy here.

109

Listing Salvageable Files

The command UNDELETE /LIST will give you a scrolling list of potentially recoverable files. Add the | More pipe to pause at each screenful, for example,

UNDELETE /DOS /LIST | MORE

Here's an example of a typical list. Files with asterisks in front of them are probably not recoverable:

```
**  ?        BAT       18   4-15-92   7:09p  ...A
**  ?        BAT       37   4-15-92   7:11p  ...A
**  ?        BAT       17   5-21-92   5:15p  ...A
**  ?B232V1D EXE   268735  12-14-92  12:45a  ...A
    ?UTOEXEC BAK      681   3-10-93   9:52a  ...A
**  ?OGO     TIF    45226  12-19-92   3:45p  ...A
**  ?NSTALL        68454  12-19-92   3:36p  ...A
    ?USTOM   TIF   81595  12-19-92   3:37p  ...A
**  ?ASIC    TIF  125014  12-19-92   3:53p  ...A
**  ?EXT     TXT        5   2-22-93  12:19p  ...A
**  ?ILE0000 CHK  2482176  2-23-93   3:13p  ....
**  ?ILE0001 CHK     4096   2-23-93   3:13p  ....
**  ?ILE0002 CHK    47104   2-23-93   3:13p  ....
**  ?ILE0003 CHK    20480   2-23-93   3:13p  ....
**  ?ILE0004 CHK    20480   2-23-93   3:13p  ....
**  ?CAN     BAT       22   2-19-93  12:48p  ...A
**  ?ILE0005 CHK    20480   2-23-93   3:13p  ....
**  ?ILE0006 CHK     2048   2-23-93   3:13p  ....

    "**" indicates the first cluster of the file
         is unavailable and cannot be recovered
         with the UNDELETE command.
 -- More --
```

Only these files are recoverable.

Which Delete-Tracking Method Is at Work?

To see which deletion-tracking method is in use, try this command at the DOS prompt:

UNDELETE /STATUS

It will tell you which method is in use (Delete Sentry, Delete Tracker, MS-DOS, or none) and which drives are protected:

```
C:\>undelete /status

UNDELETE - A delete protection facility
Copyright (C) 1987-1993 Central Point Software, Inc.
All rights reserved.

Delete Protection Method is Delete Sentry.
Enabled for drives : C D

C:\>
```

Reality Check

As you can see by now, not every deletion is recoverable, so it's best if you don't accidentally delete things. While you might be able to get them back, it's pretty iffy. Which is one of many reasons to make regular backup copies of your important stuff. That's the subject of the next lesson.

10 MINUTES

Backing Up Your Files: Preparing for the Inevitable

11

With apologies to Paul Simon, there are *at least* fifty ways to lose your data. Disk drives *all fail* sooner or later. (Reread that last sentence.) Floppy disks get damaged. People steal other peoples' computers. Much to the delight of the working press, computers are destroyed by fires, earthquakes, floods, hurricanes, tornadoes, lightning, cattle stampedes—you name it. Disgruntled ex-employees wipe out their files when they leave. Confused programs wipe out their files without meaning to. Some rascals create and distribute programs that delete data just for the heck of it (see the lesson on viruses).

Those companies housed in the World Trade Center that had effective backup procedures were up and running 24 hours after the 1993 explosion. A few of the other companies in the building that did *not* have off-site backups are no longer in business. It's that simple.

But if you are like me, you probably won't make backups—at least until the first time you've lost something really important. So skip this lesson until after your first disaster, if you like, but eventually, you'll read it.

● Note It is extremely important to develop a backup strategy, and even more important to use it religiously! It is not good enough to simply make occasional copies of your mission-critical files. You must store them away from your computer—ideally in a different zip code.

Still here? Good. The subject of backing up is worthy of a book the size of this one. What you'll read in this short lesson can get you started, but you'll probably need to become much more sophisticated as your collection of files grows. That means getting bigger books and rubbing elbows with the gurus. For now, here's the *Reader's Digest* version of some basic backup techniques.

Copying Files to Floppies

In a small business, or at home, your backup plan can be as simple as copying important files to floppy disks and taking them somewhere else. You already know how to do that. If you've forgotten, get thee to Lesson 7.

Backing Up to Other Hard Drives

Another possibility is to make copies of your files on a second hard disk—like your company's server. The problem is, unless that server or other hard disk gets backed up properly, a company-wide disaster will leave you sans files.

Some people like to use removable hard-disk cartridges made by Syquest and others for backups. It is easy to copy important files onto them, pop out the cartridges, then store them elsewhere. That's what I do.

Backing Up to Tape and Other Media

Tape drives are probably the most popular way to back up lots of files. There are many other alternatives, including "floptical" disks. A description of the merits of the various technologies could fill another book. For now, just know that if you plan to use the DOS or Windows backup features described in this chapter with other than floppy disks, be sure you purchase backup hardware that is *compatible* with the DOS 6 Backup feature. Ask before you spend.

The Windows and DOS Backup Programs

There are two DOS 6 backup programs—one for use at the DOS prompt and one for use under Windows. Only the Windows version, MWBACKUP, is installed automatically when you install DOS 6 or upgrade to DOS 6 from an earlier version. If you do not have Windows, you'll need to install and operate the MSBACKUP program, following the instructions that came with DOS.

Starting MWBACKUP

Using the Windows Program Manager, locate the Backup icon in the Microsoft Tools window, then double-click on it:

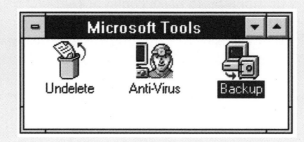

The first time you run the program it will perform a compatibility test. Be prepared with the non–write-protected media you intend to use (floppy disk, tape, etc.), and follow the instructions as the program attempts to write and recall sample files.

For instance, if you plan to back up onto 3½-inch high-density disks, have one ready and choose **B:1.44 Mb 3.5 "** in the Compatibility Test dialog box, then click on Start to run the test:

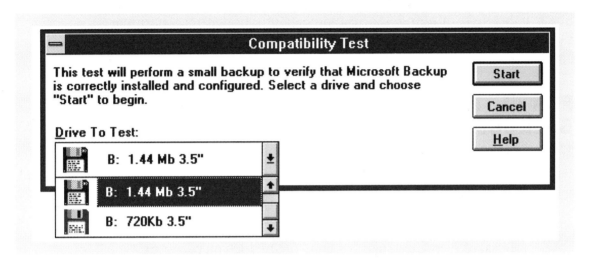

You will be prompted to insert the floppy and can watch the progress
as the test is performed:

Windows MWBACKUP Help

After the test has been run successfully, take a moment to read the on-line help before continuing. It offers some helpful background information. Use the Help menu to get started.

Full vs. Incremental and Differential Backups

You have a choice of three types of backups (Full, Incremental, and Differential). Here's an overview of what they are and why you'd want to use them:

- A *full* backup copies each and every file on your disk. It makes it easy to reinstall a copy of any file you've lost or damaged.

- An *incremental* backup records changes you've made just since the last full or incremental backup. It's quicker than a full backup and takes less space on your backup media. It can be a little confusing since you need to keep each of the incremental backups until you make another full backup.

- A *differential* backup maintains the latest versions of your files. If you only work with the same few files every day (a few databases, some bookkeeping files, etc.), this may be the most efficient choice. If you create lots of different files each day (tons of word processing documents, for instance), differential backups can get pretty big.

If you have some free time, you may want to experiment with the different choices to see which you prefer for your method of working, or check out the online help and bigger books for more insight into this topic.

Creating a Complete Hard-Disk Backup

To perform a complete hard-disk backup:

1. Run the Backup program from the Microsoft Tools window as illustrated earlier in this lesson, or activate the Backup window if the program is already running.

2. Double-click on the desired disk icon in the **Backup From:** area for the drive you wish to back up (drive C in this example).

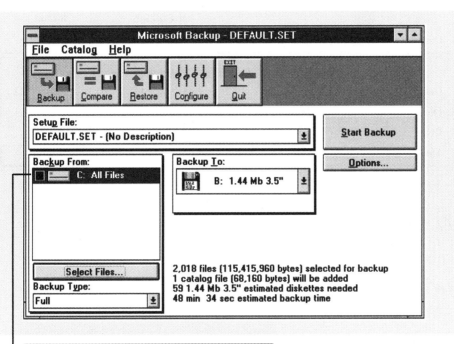

This is the drive that will be backed up.

In a moment you'll see statistics for the backup session, including number of files, total bytes, number of disks required for the backup, and an estimate of the time required (48 minutes, 34 seconds in this example).

3. Click **Start Backup** to start the backup, or choose **Exit** from the File menu if you need to run out to buy a hundred disks.

If you start the backup process, you'll be entertained and informed with colorful thermometers and statistics like this:

Backup Progress			
Now Backing Up	c:\bookfigs\figsdone		
Drive A:		**Setup**	default.set
Drive B:		**Catalog**	default.cat
Complete	22%	**Session**	cc30602a.ful

	Estimated	Actual		
Disks	3	1	**Backup Time**	0:12
Files	189	20	**Your Time**	1:02
Bytes	6,123,493	1,349,559	**Compression**	9:1
Time	2:54	1:14		Cancel

Eventually, you'll be told that the backup was successful.

Restoring from a Backup

To restore files:

1. Run the Backup program.

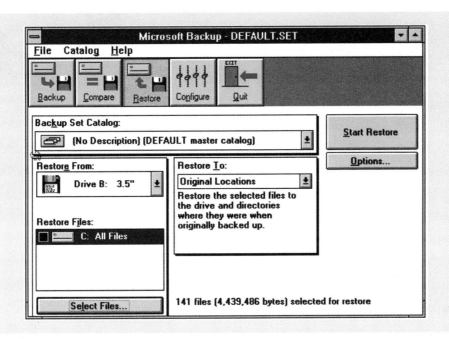

2. Select the backup set you wish to restore from.

3. Use the drop-down lists to pick the drive from which you plan to restore (B: in our example).

4. Specify the drives and files to restore. Use the **Select Files...** button if necessary.

5. Select the destination.

6. Click the **Start Restore** button.

10 MINUTES

Finding Lost Files and Directories

12

Files and subdirectories almost never just *disappear.* So the next time your computer says "Bad command or file name" or "Cannot find file Henway," and you catch yourself shouting, "This (bleeping) computer just lost my file," relax. Take a deep breath, and look carefully at what you are doing. Chances are that your problem was caused by one or more of the following:

- You've mistyped a file's name or path.

- You've forgotten a file's name or location.

- You are logged onto the wrong disk drive.

- You have the wrong floppy in a disk drive.

- You are using the wrong View options in the Shell or Windows File Manager.

- You or someone else has moved the file or subdirectory.

- You don't have the appropriate access privileges for the network file you are attempting to use.

- The file has been accidentally or intentionally deleted.

Typing errors are easy to fix. Either retype the entire command or use the **F1** and **F3** function keys (described in Lesson 16) to redisplay and edit the erroneous command.

If you don't have the right network access privilege, you'll need to get help from the network manager or perhaps from the file's "owner."

If files or subdirectories have been deleted, you can try the techniques described in Lesson 10 to recover them.

But, if you think you've just forgotten a name or path—or if someone has moved or renamed things—DOS can help you do some detective work.

Searching for Lost Files from the DOS Prompt

You already know how to look for things with the DOS DIR command, described in earlier lessons. For instance, if you want to find all the files on your hard disk that end with the extension TXT, the command

    DIR *.TXT /S /P

will search all your subdirectories, fill your screen with "hits," and pause. The /S switch also shows the names of the subdirectories containing the files. Here's an example of that:

```
 Volume in drive C is AST_RON'S
 Volume Serial Number is 1A8F-7A43

Directory of C:\ADAM\SBPRO

README    TXT       7104 11-19-91    3:09p
          1 file(s)        7104 bytes

Directory of C:\ADAM\SBPRO\SBTALKER

SBTEST    TXT         32 06-13-90   10:38a
          1 file(s)          32 bytes

Directory of C:\ADAM\SBPRO\VEDIT2

VOC2WAV   TXT       3477 12-02-91    1:59p
          1 file(s)        3477 bytes

Directory of C:\DOS

NETWORKS TXT       23444 03-10-93    6:00a
README    TXT      61857 03-10-93    6:00a
OS2       TXT       6358 03-10-93    6:00a
Press any key to continue . . .
```

While creating the illustrations for Lesson 11, I tried to run a file called
MSBACKUP.EXE. I kept getting the message "Bad command or file
name." So I used the command

    DIR ??BACK??.* /S

to look for it. Here's what happened:

```
C:\>DIR ??BACK??.* /S

 Volume in drive C is AST_RON'S
 Volume Serial Number is 1A8F-7A43

Directory of C:\DOS

MWBACKUP EXE      309696 03-10-93   6:00a
MWBACKUP HLP      400880 03-10-93   6:00a
MWBACKF  DLL       14560 03-10-93   6:00a
MWBACKR  DLL      111120 03-10-93   6:00a
         4 file(s)      836256 bytes

Directory of C:\WINDOWS

MWBACKUP INI         376 04-18-93  10:31a
         1 file(s)         376 bytes

Total files listed:
         5 file(s)      836632 bytes
                      20404224 bytes free

C:\>
```

I found the *Windows* version of the backup program
(MWBACKUP.EXE) but not the DOS version (MSBACKUP.EXE).
So, I popped one of the DOS 6 installation disks into drive B, changed
the path to include the drive name, and searched again with only
slightly better luck:

```
MSBACKFB OVL       69066 03-10-93   6:00a
MSBACKFR OVL       72474 03-10-93   6:00a
MSBACKUP EX_        2487 03-10-93   6:00a
MSBACKUP OVL      133952 03-10-93   6:00a
MWBACKF  DL_        6956 03-10-93   6:00a
MWBACKR  DL_       30277 03-10-93   6:00a
MWBACKUP EX_      159138 03-10-93   6:00a
MWBACKUP HL_      141281 03-10-93   6:00a
```

This time I found a file name that was close (MSBACKUP.EX_),
but it didn't have exactly the right extension, at which point I called
Microsoft for advice. It seems that the installer only installs the
Windows version of the backup program (MWBACKUP) if you have
Windows on your hard disk. And it changes the extension from
EX_ to EXE when you install the DOS version.

Searching from the Shell

Similar searches can be performed from within the Shell:

1. With the Shell running, choose **Search**... from the File menu.

2. Enter the search request in the Search File dialog box. In
this example, **??BACK??.*** has been entered.

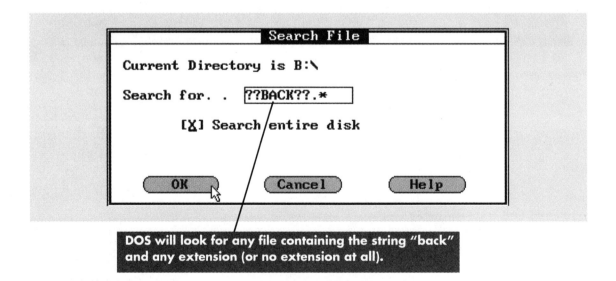

**DOS will look for any file containing the string "back"
and any extension (or no extension at all).**

3. Be sure there's an X in the **Search entire disk** check box if
that's what you want to do (point and click to add or remove the X).

4. Click OK or press ↵ to start the search. Soon you will see a window containing "hits":

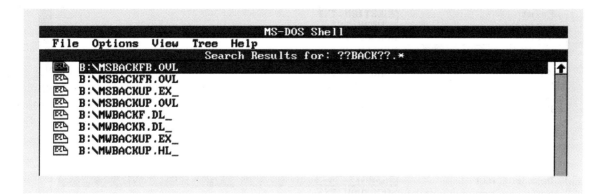

```
                            MS-DOS Shell
 File   Options   View   Tree   Help
                     Search Results for: ??BACK??.*
     B:\MSBACKFB.OVL                                             ⬆
     B:\MSBACKFR.OVL
     B:\MSBACKUP.EX_
     B:\MSBACKUP.OVL
     B:\MWBACKF.DL_
     B:\MWBACKR.DL_
     B:\MWBACKUP.EX_
     B:\MWBACKUP.HL_
```

5. Scroll, if necessary, to see them all.

Examining the Contents of Files with the Shell

It is often useful to be able to view the *contents* of found files. This can be a big help when someone has renamed word processing or other files containing text.

1. Use the Shell's Search command to round up files, as described previously.

2. Select a file of interest by clicking on it.

3. Choose **View File Contents** from the Shell's File menu or press **F9**.

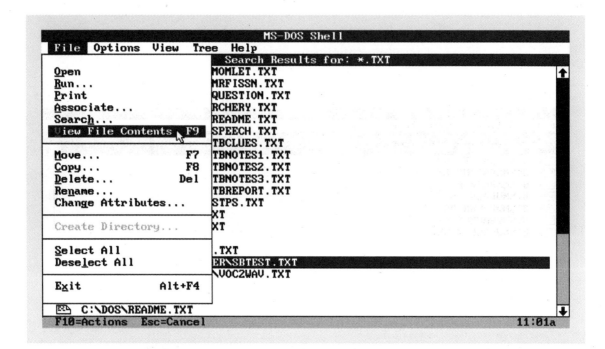

You will see the beginning of the file in a window. It may or may not look like everyday text. If you are lucky, you'll see something like this:

4. To see more of the file, press Page Down.

5. When you have finished looking at the file, press Esc to return to the main Shell screen.

What do you do if your file looks like this when you first view it?

```
                     MS-DOS Shell - README.TXT
  Display  View  Help
        ew file's content use PgUp or PgDn or ↑ or ↓.
  Ascii
  Hex          0D0A2020   20202020   20202020   20202020    ..
              20202053   4F554E44   20424C41   53544552       SOUND BLASTER
  000020      2050524F   20204C41   54455354   20494E46    PRO  LATEST INF
  000030      4F524D41   54494F4E   0D0A2020   20202020    ORMATION..
  000040      20202020   20202020   2020203D   3D3D3D3D              =====
  000050      3D3D3D3D   3D3D3D3D   3D3D3D3D   3D3D3D3D    ================
  000060      3D3D3D3D   3D3D3D3D   3D3D3D3D   3D3D3D3D    ================
  000070      0D0A0D0A   312E2020   494E5354   414C4C41    ....1.   INSTALLA
  000080      54494F4E   0D0A0D0A   41206861   72642064    TION....A hard d
  000090      69736B20   69732072   65717569   72656420    isk is required
```

Either press the F9 key to display text or choose the ASCII option from the Display menu. Not all files will be readable, even after you have done this.

Finding Lost Files with the Windows File Manager

The Windows File Manager has a search feature that works a lot like the Shell's.

To view the contents of files, double-click on them and Windows will attempt to open them with Notepad, a small word-processing accessory. You will either see the file or a message saying that Notepad can't open it.

Finding Lost Directories

You already know how to find lost directories. Refer back to Lesson 4 if you need to refresh your memory. Use the DOS TREE command or expand directory views in the Shell or the Windows File Manager.

Learning More

What should you know about the care and feeding of floppy disks? Have you discovered the various online help features provided by DOS? Are there some easy DOS tricks that can make you more productive? What should you be doing about virus protection, and how can DOS 6 help? What's all the fuss about DoubleSpace, and should you use it? Part Three holds the answers.

10 MINUTES

The Care and Feeding of Floppy Disks

13

Usually, you'll be working with data on your hard disk, or perhaps on a network server. But once in a while, you'll need to deal with floppy disks. You will use them to install new software. You may copy files onto floppies to give them to a coworker or to take them to another computer. And, if you don't have a tape drive or other high-capacity backup device, you'll be using floppies to store backup copies of important files.

While today's floppy disks (also called *removable media*) are quite reliable, they need to be handled and stored carefully to prevent accidental data loss or corruption. This lesson looks at selecting, preparing, using, and protecting floppy disks.

Buying the Right Disks

Over the years computer manufacturers have developed a variety of disk-drive and floppy-disk standards. Floppy disks usually come in one of two sizes—$5\frac{1}{4}$-inch or $3\frac{1}{2}$-inch. It's pretty obvious by looking at the floppy-drive slots on your computer which *size* disks you can use. Unfortunately, there's another variable.

Some disk drives can store more information on a disk than others can. These drives require disks with different magnetic coatings. For instance, some $3\frac{1}{2}$-inch drives can store only 720,000 bytes (720K) of information per disk and require "double-density" (also called "low-density") disks; others can store a million or more bytes and require "quadruple-density" (also called "high-density") disks.

Generally, newer machines use the higher-density disks and store between 720K (720,000 bytes) and 2.8MB (2,800,000 bytes) per disk. (Incidentally, a byte is the *very* rough equivalent of a character.)

Consult your computer manual, dealer, or guru if you are unsure of the types of disks you can use with your computer. Here is a list of the common disk standards in use today. Make a note of the ones your computer can use.

- 360K, double-sided, double-density, 5$\frac{1}{4}$-inch disk

- 720K, double-sided, double-density, 3$\frac{1}{2}$-inch disk

- 1.2MB, double-sided, high-density, 5$\frac{1}{4}$-inch disk

- 1.44MB, double-sided, high-density, 3$\frac{1}{2}$-inch disk

- 2.88MB, double-sided, extra-high-density, 3$\frac{1}{2}$-inch disk

The 1.2MB and 1.44MB drives are commonly found in newer computers.

You can generally read lower-capacity disks in high-capacity drives, but it is a very bad idea to try to write to them with the wrong drive type. Whenever possible, use the right kind of disks for your drives.

 **● Note** When shopping for floppy disks, avoid incredibly low priced ones. While most disks come from one of a half-dozen or so disk makers, regardless of brand name, very cheap disks may be unreliable or cause damage to your drives. To save money, buy "bulk" packages of name-brand disks from discounters.

Telling Disk Types on Sight

When purchasing new blank disks, read the box carefully, and keep them in their original packaging. If you are holding a "mystery disk" in your hand, you can sometimes tell its capacity from the label on the disk. If it is a $3\frac{1}{2}$-inch disk, you can tell that it is high-density if it has a second square hole in the upper-left corner. If it is a $5\frac{1}{4}$-inch disk, you can tell that it is high-density if it does not have a black ring around the hub in the middle. (Take a look at the illustrations at the end of this lesson.)

Formatting Floppy Disks

Before disks can accept data they need to be prepared, or "formatted." You can purchase preformatted disks, or you can buy unformatted disks and format them yourself with DOS. Expect to spend a dime or less per disk for preformatted ones. It's an affordable, quick-and-easy luxury.

You can format disks from the DOS prompt, from the Shell, or from the Windows File Manager. Let's start with the Shell approach.

Formatting Disks with the Shell

To format a disk with the Shell, first make sure that the Main pane is showing by selecting Program List from the View menu.

1. Choose [Disk Utilities].

2. Choose Format. You'll see the Format dialog box.

3. Type in the drive letter for the disk you want to format, and choose OK.

● Note The Quick Format option is for people who are in a hurry when formatting their disks. Don't you be one of them. Take your time. Let DOS check for defects on your disks. Throw out defective disks, or get a refund on new ones that don't format properly.

Formatting Disks with Windows

To format disks with the Windows File Manager, you simply choose Format Disk... from the Disk menu. The dialog box that comes up has more options than the equivalent one in the Shell. You can specify the density by using the drop-down list.

The DOS FORMAT Command

To format a disk from the DOS prompt with the DOS FORMAT command, at a minimum you'll need to specify the drive letter. You can only get away with this easily if the disk you use matches the formatting capacity of the selected drive. For instance, if you are using a B: drive designed to format 1.44MB disks, and you insert a 1.44MB disk, follow these steps:

1. Insert a non–write-protected disk of the proper capacity in drive B.

2. At the DOS prompt, type FORMAT B: and press ↵.

DOS will ask you to put a disk in drive B (even though there's already one there) and press ↵.

```
C:\>format b:
Insert new diskette for drive B:
and press ENTER when ready...
```

3. Press ↵ to start the formatting. DOS will appraise you of its progress (the exact messages may vary somewhat), then it will ask for a disk label.

4. Type an optional disk name of up to eleven letters and numbers (no spaces or other funny stuff).

5. Press ↵.

```
Checking existing disk format.
Formatting 1.44M
Format complete.

Volume label (11 characters, ENTER for none)? PTA_BACKUPS
```

6. DOS will tell you things you never wanted to know about a disk and ask if you want to format another. A simple Y or N will do here. Press ↵ to continue.

```
   1457664 bytes total disk space
   1457664 bytes available on disk

      512 bytes in each allocation unit.
     2847 allocation units available on disk.

Volume Serial Number is 3A49-16E0

Format another (Y/N)?
```

There are a number of FORMAT command switches that you can read about in online help or in the bigger books.

Oops? Try the UNFORMAT Command

DOS offers an UNFORMAT command, which you'll never need to use if you are careful. But if you accidentally format your favorite disk, this is worth a try, particularly if you catch the mistake before you copy new stuff to the disk.

1. Insert the accidentally formatted disk in the drive.

2. At the DOS prompt, type UNFORMAT and the drive name (UNFORMAT B:, for instance).

3. Press ↵.

4. DOS will wonder if that's what you really want to do. Type Y and press ↵ to start the unformatting attempt. Soon you will learn your fate:

```
Restores the system area of your disk by using the image file created
by the MIRROR command.

    WARNING !!          WARNING !!

This command should be used only to recover from the inadvertent use of
the FORMAT command or the RECOVER command.  Any other use of the UNFORMAT
command may cause you to lose data!  Files modified since the MIRROR image
file was created may be lost.

Searching disk for MIRROR image.

The last time the MIRROR or FORMAT command was used was at 16:02 on 04-19-93.

The MIRROR image file has been validated.

Are you sure you want to update the system area of your drive B (Y/N)? y

The system area of drive B has been rebuilt.

You may need to restart the system.

C:\>
```

Don't worry about what the Mirror command does. DOS uses the results of this command to help with unformatting the disk.

Normally you will not need to restart the computer after restoring files on floppies, DOS's warning notwithstanding.

Caring for Your Floppies

Organize and store your disks out of harm's way. Magnets, heat, liquids, and carelessness are disks' worst enemies. Computer consultants love those little paper-clip dispensers you all have on your desks. Many of them have huge magnets in them. Pass a disk nearby (or better still, put a box of your favorite disks next to a magnet) and there is a very good chance that some or all of your data will be unusable. Ban magnets from your desktop. No "I Love My Hubby" refrigerator magnets, no paper-clip dispensers, no magnetic screwdrivers in the briefcase, no boombox nearby—you get the picture.

Keep disks out of direct sunlight, and never store them in cars exposed to sunlight with the windows rolled up.

Keep 5¼-inch disks in their sleeves when you're not using them. Don't touch the magnetic part of disks (the "insides") with your fingers.

It takes a long time to create data, but only a careless second or two to destroy it. End of sermon.

Write-Protecting Floppies

To prevent programs and DOS itself from accidentally changing the contents of disks, you can "write-protect" them. Write-protect a 3½-inch disk by sliding the little plastic square to open the square on the right side of the disk as you view it from the front:

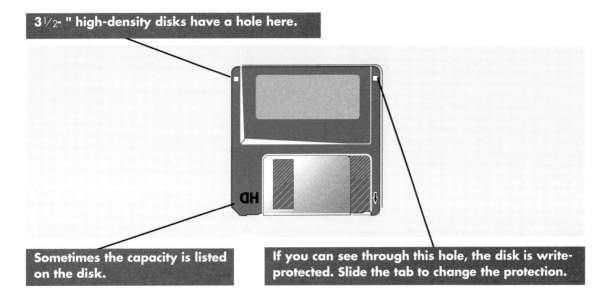

3 1/2- " high-density disks have a hole here.

Sometimes the capacity is listed on the disk.

If you can see through this hole, the disk is write-protected. Slide the tab to change the protection.

Write-protect a 5¼-inch disk by placing an adhesive "tab" over the notch on the right side:

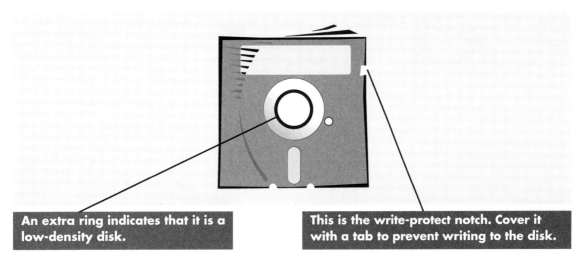

An extra ring indicates that it is a low-density disk.

This is the write-protect notch. Cover it with a tab to prevent writing to the disk.

In the next lesson, you'll learn all about getting help.

10 MINUTES

Getting Help

14

There are plenty of ways to get online help when you have questions about DOS 6, the Shell, or Windows. In fact, there is even help for the Help features (thanks to Microsoft's department of redundancy department). When the computer can't tell you what you need to know, you can often pick up the phone and talk to a human, or use your fax machine to get printed assistance. If your computer has a modem, Microsoft's electronic bulletin board service (BBS) may have the answers. Let's take a look at the bewildering world of help.

Getting Quick Help with the /? Switch

Simply typing the name of a DOS command and the switch /? then pressing ↵ at the DOS prompt can often tell you what you need to know. For instance, suppose you have forgotten some of the switches you can use with the DIR command. By simply typing DIR/? and pressing ↵, you'll see a screen like the one on the next page.

```
Displays a list of files and subdirectories in a directory.

DIR [drive:][path][filename] [/P] [/W] [/A[[:]attribs]] [/O[[:]sortord]]
   [/S] [/B] [/L] [/C[H]]

  [drive:][path][filename]   Specifies drive, directory, and/or files to list.
  /P       Pauses after each screenful of information.
  /W       Uses wide list format.
  /A       Displays files with specified attributes.
  attribs   D  Directories    R  Read-only files       H  Hidden files
            S  System files   A  Files ready to archive -  Prefix meaning "not"
  /O       List by files in sorted order.
  sortord   N  By name (alphabetic)        S  By size (smallest first)
            E  By extension (alphabetic)   D  By date & time (earliest first)
            G  Group directories first     -  Prefix to reverse order
            C  By compression ratio (smallest first)
  /S       Displays files in specified directory and all subdirectories.
  /B       Uses bare format (no heading information or summary).
  /L       Uses lowercase.
  /C[H]    Displays file compression ratio; /CH uses host allocation unit size.

Switches may be preset in the DIRCMD environment variable.  Override
preset switches by prefixing any switch with - (hyphen)--for example, /-W.

C:\>
```

Notice that this technique returns you to the DOS prompt, so you can continue to work immediately without first "quitting" Help. It's quick and easy. It's the perfect way to jog your memory. There is no need to type a space between the command name and the /? switch, but it's OK if you do.

If you type a nonexistent command (like CLEAR) or make a typo (like DIRR), DOS will respond with the message "Bad command or file name." Either retype the command correctly or use the HELP command, described next, to get a list of valid DOS commands.

Using the DOS HELP Command

This second DOS Help feature requires you to type the word **HELP**, and *optionally* the name of the command that you need help with. For

example, you could either type HELP DIR then press ↵ or simply type HELP then press ↵. If you type HELP and the name of a valid DOS command, you'll be taken directly to a Help screen for that command. Otherwise, you'll see an index of commands.

For instance, here's what you see if you type HELP DIR and tap ↵:

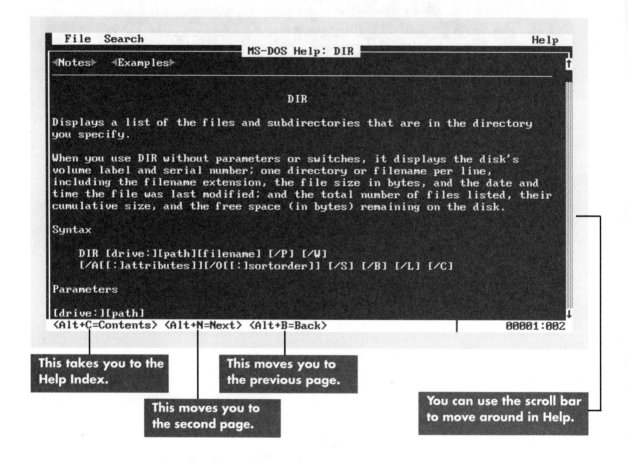

Your screen will display the first page of help for the chosen topic (the DIR command in our example). The bottom of the screen shows you the keyboard shortcuts for moving forward and backward (Alt-N and Alt-B). It also shows you that pressing the Alt-C combination will take you to the index—a list of help topics.

Scrolling in the Help Window

The usual scroll keys work with the Help feature. For instance, Page Up, Page Down, and the arrow keys can be used to scroll text in Help windows. Pressing Tab moves you to additional topics, which you can read by pressing ↵. You can also use your mouse to scroll by pointing and clicking on the scroll bars at the right edge of the screen.

Choosing Help Topics

If you just type HELP at the DOS prompt and press ↵, or if you choose Contents (Alt-C) while using the DOS Help feature, you'll see a list of help topics like this:

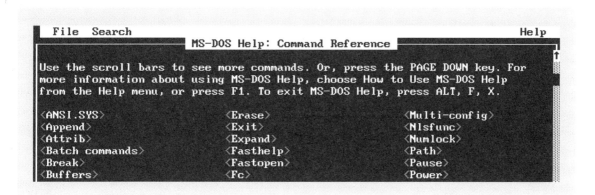

```
 File   Search                                                      Help
                      MS-DOS Help: Command Reference
                                                                        ↑
Use the scroll bars to see more commands. Or, press the PAGE DOWN key. For
more information about using MS-DOS Help, choose How to Use MS-DOS Help
from the Help menu, or press F1. To exit MS-DOS Help, press ALT, F, X.

<ANSI.SYS>                 <Erase>                    <Multi-config>
<Append>                   <Exit>                      <Nlsfunc>
<Attrib>                   <Expand>                    <Numlock>
<Batch commands>           <Fasthelp>                  <Path>
<Break>                    <Fastopen>                  <Pause>
<Buffers>                  <Fc>                        <Power>
```

You select a topic by moving the cursor to the topic and pressing ↵ or F1. Move the cursor by pointing and clicking with your mouse or by pressing Tab, which will cause the cursor to march from one topic to the next. If you press Shift-Tab, the cursor will move backward. Arrow keys will also move the cursor. Or, if you type the first letter of a command, the cursor will move to the first command that starts with that letter (for example, *Keyb* if you type K).

Read the instructions at the top of the screen if you forget how to navigate in this rather cluttered window.

Searching DOS Help Text for Words You're Interested In

What if you don't remember the exact name of the command that clears the screen, or you remember reading something about clearing the screen, but don't know where in Help you read it? You can search the help text itself.

1. Use your mouse to choose the **Find...** command from the Search menu at the top of the Help window, or use the Alt-S F keyboard shortcut. You'll see the Find dialog box.

2. In the Find What: box, type in a word or words that you wish to find (clear, for example).

```
┌──────────────────────── Find ────────────────────────┐
│                                                       │
│  Find What: │clear                                  │ │
│                                                       │
│                                                       │
│   [ ] Match Upper/Lowercase          [ ] Whole Word  │
│                                                       │
│   < OK >            < Cancel >           < Help >     │
└───────────────────────────────────────────────────────┘
```

3. Click OK or press ↵ to begin the search. DOS will display the first occurrence of the requested text.

4. If that's not the help you need, press F3 to see the next occurrence.

5. Keep pressing F3 until you see what you want—the CLS command in our example:

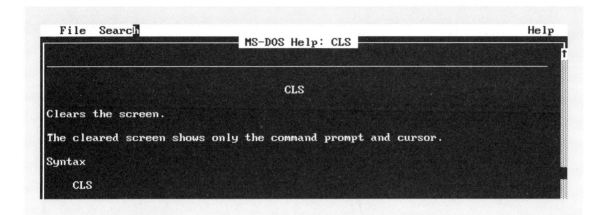

```
   File  Search                                                    Help
                          MS-DOS Help: CLS
                                                                         ↑

                                    CLS
Clears the screen.

The cleared screen shows only the command prompt and cursor.

Syntax

     CLS
```

● Note In step 2 you can further restrict the search to show only complete word matches with specific capitalization by selecting Whole Word and Match Upper/Lowercase. It's usually not a good idea to do that, since you may miss something of interest.

Printing DOS Help Screen Information

If you want a paper copy of on-screen help:

1. Display the information of interest.

2. Make sure your printer is ready.

3. Use your mouse to choose the Print... command from the Help window's File menu with your mouse, or use the Alt-F P key combination. You'll see a Print dialog box like the one on the following page.

143

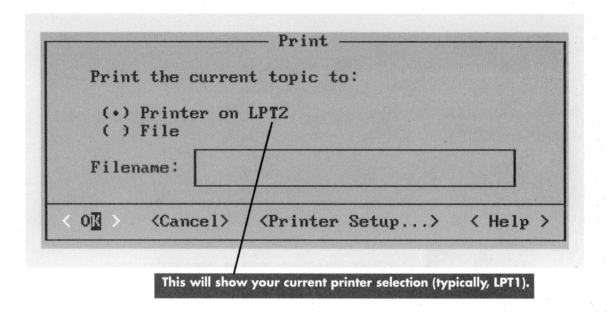

```
┌──────────────────────── Print ─────────────────────────┐
│                                                         │
│   Print the current topic to:                           │
│                                                         │
│     (•) Printer on LPT2                                 │
│     ( ) File                                            │
│                                                         │
│     Filename: ┌─────────────────────────────────────┐  │
│               │                                     │  │
│               └─────────────────────────────────────┘  │
│                                                         │
│  < OK >    <Cancel>   <Printer Setup...>   < Help >    │
└─────────────────────────────────────────────────────────┘
```

This will show your current printer selection (typically, LPT1).

4. Use your mouse or the Tab key to change the choices if
necessary.

5. Finally, click OK or press ↵ to print the help information.

Exiting the DOS Help Window

To quit the DOS Help feature, use your mouse to pick the Exit command from the File menu, or press Alt-F X.

Shell Help

Shell has its own online help, which you can access by pressing the
F1 function key. The Shell also has a Help menu containing six help-
related choices.

When you press F1, the Shell will attempt to give you context-sensitive
help. For instance, if the file-list portion of the Shell window is active

when you press F1, you'll see a screen like this describing the file list:

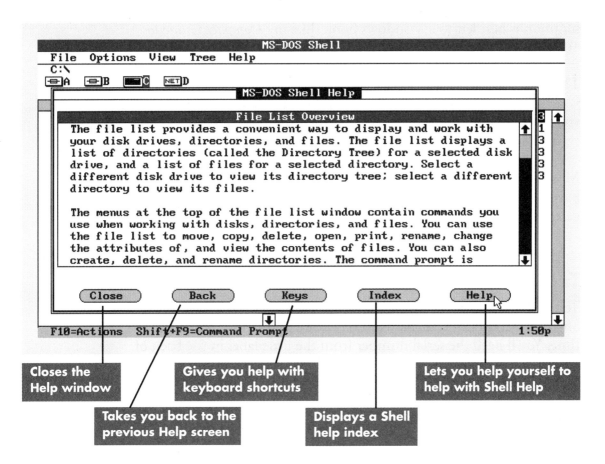

Closes the Help window

Gives you help with keyboard shortcuts

Lets you help yourself to help with Shell Help

Takes you back to the previous Help screen

Displays a Shell help index

Many of the usual navigation tools work here (your mouse, Page Up, Page Down, and the arrow keys, for instance), but the Tab key serves a slightly different purpose than it does in DOS command Help windows. Pressing Tab or Shift-Tab lets you use the buttons in the Shell windows without a mouse.

As you press Tab, notice how the little "cursor thingie" moves from button to button. When you've selected the button you want to use, press ↵ to "click" the button.

Windows Help

There are several Windows online help features, too. While a full description is best left to a Windows book (like my *Compact Guide to Windows, Word & Excel,* SYBEX, 1992), here's an overview.

The F1 key attempts to give you context-sensitive help based on what you are doing. For instance, if you're in the File Manager and press F1, you'll get help on File Manager-related topics. In Word for Windows, the F1 key gives you Word help.

Most programs (including Windows utilities like Program Manager) have Help menus. Check out the help index in each program and navigate as you would in the Shell.

Telephone Help

To reach a Microsoft product support person about DOS 6 or the Shell, dial 206-646-5104 between 6:00 a.m. and 6:00 p.m. Pacific time. You'll need the serial number from the little label in the back of your Microsoft DOS 6 manual the first time you call. You may find BBS or FastTips (fax) services quicker for "common" problems.

Other Kinds of Help

If you have a modem-equipped computer and communications software, you can use them to get help with your problems and to "download" useful files from Microsoft. Have your modem dial 206-936-6735.

If you have a fax machine and some patience, you can use an automated fax service to receive written solutions to common DOS 6 problems. Dial 206-646-5103 and follow the spoken instructions. It has been my (admittedly limited) experience that you can get the same information more quickly and reliably from the BBS.

For the hearing impaired, TDD/TT (Text Telephone) help is available by dialing 206-635-4948.

15

More DOS Commands You Should Know

Computers are like the game of chess. You can learn enough to start enjoying yourself in a few hours, then spend a lifetime becoming a master. This lesson introduces you to a few DOS commands you don't really need to know but may find interesting and helpful.

Setting Your Computer's Clock with DATE and TIME

DOS and some of your programs use your computer's built-in clock/calendar chip to date-stamp files, insert dates and times in reports, and so on.

There's a little battery in your computer that keeps the clock running even if your computer is turned off or unplugged. Occasionally, however, you'll want to check or change the date and time—to spring ahead or fall back, for instance. The DOS DATE and TIME commands do this. Use them one at a time.

Checking and Changing the Time

1. At the DOS prompt, type TIME and press ↵. You'll see the time your computer thinks it is.

2. If the time is OK, press ↵.

3. To change the time, enter a new time in the format *hours:minutes:seconds.hundredths* (leading zeros, minutes, seconds, and hundredths are all optional).

4. Specify a.m. or p.m. with a or p (9:a, for example, for 9 a.m.).

5. Press ↵ to set the clock.

```
C:\>time
Current time is  8:59:32.04a
Enter new time: 9:a
```

Checking and Changing the Date

1. At the DOS prompt, type DATE and press ↵. You'll see the date your computer thinks it is.

2. If the date is OK, press ↵.

3. To change the date, enter a new date in the format *mm-dd-yy* (04-24-93, for instance). Zeros are optional.

4. Press ↵ to set the date.

```
C:\>date
Current date is Fri 04-23-1993
Enter new date (mm-dd-yy): 04-24-93
```

If you are a collector of antique computers and classic books, and if you are reading this in the year 2000 or later, gently type the *complete* year on your pride-and-joy (2001, for example).

Use online help to learn more about things like 24-hour and international date options. (Type HELP TIME or HELP DATE at the DOS prompt.)

Changing the Appearance of Your DOS Prompt with PROMPT

If you haven't done so already, you'll probably want to change the appearance of the DOS prompt to show the path to the current directory you are logged into. Do this by typing

```
PROMPT $P$G
```

There are other PROMPT options, all explained in online help (type HELP PROMPT). Some people like to add text to their prompts— like the text in the last part of the example below. This is the computer wonk's version of vanity license plates, I suppose.

```
C>prompt $p$g

C:\>prompt What now, oh great one?$g

What now, oh great one?>
```

Reading Text Files on the Screen with TYPE

While both the Shell and Windows provide text-editing tools that can be used to read text files, there's an old DOS command that, when coupled with the More pipe, provides a quick way to read a text file. Suppose, for instance, you want to read the README.TXT file on an MS-DOS 6 upgrade floppy disk in your B: drive.

1. Insert the disk.

2. Enter the command

   TYPE B:\README.TXT | MORE

3. Press ↵. You'll see the first page of text.

4. Press the **spacebar** or nearly any other key to see more text, or press **Ctrl-C** to quit reading.

```
README.TXT

NOTES ON MS-DOS 6
=================

This file provides important information not included in the
MICROSOFT MS-DOS 6 USER'S GUIDE or in MS-DOS Help.

This file is divided into the following major sections:

1. Setup
2. MemMaker and Memory Management
3. Windows
4. Hardware Compatibility with MS-DOS 6
5. Microsoft Programs
6. Third-Party Programs
7. DoubleSpace

If the subject you need information about doesn't appear in
this file, you might find it in one of the following text
files included with MS-DOS:

* OS2.TXT, which describes how to remove and save data on your
-- More --
```

Learning and Changing Volume Names with LABEL

To see, and optionally change, the name of a *volume* (the name of a disk):

1. Type LABEL and optionally the drive name (B:, for instance).

2. Press ↵. The current drive name will be displayed.

```
C:\>label
Volume in drive C is AST_RON'S
Volume Serial Number is 1A8F-7A43
Volume label (11 characters, ENTER for none)?
```

3. Type a new name if you like, or just press ↵.

4. You'll have the choice of deleting the current name or keeping it (type Y or N and press ↵).

If your computer is on a network, or if someone has set up an automatic backup procedure for you, check with someone knowledgeable before renaming your hard disk this way. It may cause problems.

Checking the DOS Version Number with VER

The VER command is handy when you walk up to someone else's computer and wonder which version of DOS is installed (not all DOS versions have the same features). The VER command will tell you which version of DOS is at work. Simply type VER and tap ↵. You'll see a no-frills report like this:

```
C:\>ver

MS-DOS Version 6.00
```

Getting Hardware Technical Info with MSD

MSD (Microsoft Diagnostics) is a fascinating command I'll mention since you can learn a lot about your computer with it if you are a "computer-person wannabe." It is also helpful when someone is working with you to over the phone troubleshoot a problem. The MSD command checks your computer's innards and reports back.

1. Start by typing MSD and pressing ↵ at the DOS prompt.

MSD will inspect your computer and perhaps mention a problem it has found, but it will not correct the problem. You will also see a screen like the one on the following page.

Quick&Easy

```
 File  Utilities  Help

    Computer...█       AST/IBM              Disk Drives...    A: B: C:
                       486DX

    Memory...          640K, 3328K Ext,     LPT Ports...      1
                       1932K XMS

    Video...           VGA, AST             COM Ports...      2
                       Integra

    Network...         No Network           IRQ Status...

    OS Version...      MS-DOS Version 6.00  TSR Programs...

    Mouse...           PS/2 Style Mouse     Device Drivers...
                       6.26

  Other Adapters...    Game Adapter

 Press ALT for menu, or press highlighted letter, or F3 to quit MSD.
```

2. Clicking on the various topics with your mouse will bring up information about your computer. Here's the scoop on my video adapter, for instance:

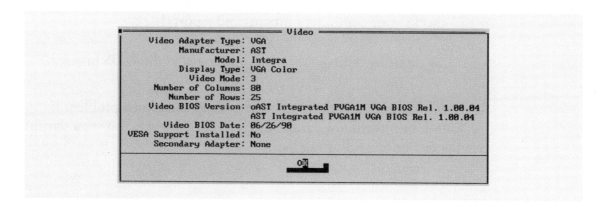

```
 ═══════════════════════════ Video ═══════════════════════════
       Video Adapter Type: VGA
             Manufacturer: AST
                    Model: Integra
             Display Type: VGA Color
               Video Mode: 3
        Number of Columns: 80
           Number of Rows: 25
       Video BIOS Version: oAST Integrated PVGA1M VGA BIOS Rel. 1.00.04
                           AST Integrated PVGA1M VGA BIOS Rel. 1.00.04
          Video BIOS Date: 06/26/90
   VESA Support Installed: No
        Secondary Adapter: None

                         ─────  OK  ─────
```

Click OK when you're finished reading the screen.

3. The File and Utilities menus list other tests and reports, which technicians may ask you to use. Reveal them with your mouse or use the Alt and arrow keys as usual.

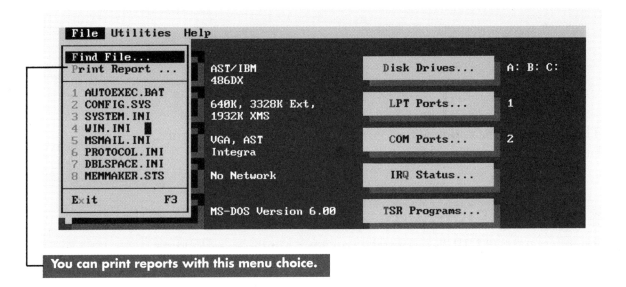

You can print reports with this menu choice.

4. To quite MSD, press F3.

That's it from Wonkland, readers. Now for something we hope you'll really like: quick tricks and tips.

5 MINUTES

DOS Tricks Worth Learning

There are lots of shortcuts built into DOS. They can save time and take the "Grrrrr" out of computing—particularly at the DOS prompt. Here are some of *my* favorites.

Stopping Runaway Actions with Ctrl-C

You say you typed DIR /S by mistake and your computer is plodding through a never-ending list of files? To stop it (or many other seemingly endless operations), try holding down Ctrl while pressing C. This has been the galaxy-wide shortcut for "Stop that!" since computers were invented. It even works from within programs sometimes. Try it. Maybe you'll get lucky.

```
Directory of C:\ADAM\SBPRO\DRV

.               <DIR>       03-09-93    6:36p
..              <DIR>       03-09-93    6:36p
CT-VOICE  DRV         5124  11-29-91   10:30a
ORGAN     DRV          506  06-23-91   12:38p
CTVDSK    DRV         7800  12-04-91   12:05p
        5 file(s)          13430 bytes

Directory of C:\ADAM\SBPRO\MIDI

.               <DIR>       03-09-93    6:37p
..              <DIR>       03-09-93    6:37p
BALLAD2   MID         7428  03-13-91   11:50a
JAZZ3     MID        14198  03-13-91   11:51a
MINUET1   MID         1851  11-26-90    9:09a
REGGAE2   MID        12084  03-13-91   11:51a
^C      6 file(s)          35561 bytes

C:\>
```

Pressing **Ctrl-C** stops the current activity and displays ^C.

Warm-Booting Your Computer with Ctrl-Alt-Delete

Have you ever read the instruction "Warm boot your computer" or maybe "restart" your computer? Or has your machine completely locked up—seemingly possessed by demons or the devil? After consulting your manuals and guru, try holding down three keys at once—Ctrl-Alt-Delete. This will usually reset your computer and bring it back to life.

● Note If you have programs running and files open, use Ctrl-Alt-Delete *only as a last resort* unless instructed to do so in a manual or by a whiz. It is *always* best to quit (exit) all programs properly before restarting with Ctrl-Alt-Delete. Otherwise you might damage your files.

Beating the "Abort, Retry, Fail?" Runaround

The DOS message "Abort, Retry, Fail?" is so universally loathed and joked about that it is used as the title of a famous computer column that focuses on the absurd and frustrating aspects of computing. In early versions of DOS, there were virtually no ways out of this trap— no right answer, if you will.

At some point in your life you *will* see the message. It generally appears for one of five reasons:

- You forgot to put a disk in a floppy drive.

- You put in a floppy but forgot to flip the latch.

- The disk is unformatted.

- The disk you are trying to use is damaged or defective.

- You're having a bad hair day.

If you forgot to load the disk, put it in, and if the drive has a latch (all $5\frac{1}{4}$-inch drives have latches), check it. Then type R for retry.

In any other case, the best thing to do is to type **F** for fail, then type the name of a known working disk drive (C: in this example).

```
C:\>b:

Not ready reading drive B
Abort, Retry, Fail?f
Current drive is no longer valid>C:

C:\>
```

Type a valid drive name and press ⏎ to escape the "Abort, Retry, Fail?" trap.

You'll see the DOS prompt and have a chance to format that disk, re-place it, or fix your hair.

Switching to the Root Directory Quickly

You say you are way out there in C:\MEMOS\ADMIN\HEALTH\FEMALE land and you want to return to the root directory? Simply type

CD\

and press ⏎.

● Note You can type CD.. to go back up one level in the tree—in this case, to C:\MEMOS\ADMIN\HEALTH.

Using the F1 and F3 Keys to Save Time at the DOS Prompt

Sometimes it's useful to reuse parts of the previous DOS command without retyping it. Let's use an almost trivial example to illustrate the concept. Suppose you've just used the DIR B: command and want to

type DIR C:. Instead of retyping the command, you can press **F1** four times to redisplay the first four characters (DIR and a space), type the replacement drive letter (C in our example), and then press **F1** again to reuse the colon from the previous command.

You can use the **F3** key to redisplay your last DOS command in its entirety.

17

Batch Files: Automating DOS Commands

Batch files are simply little programs that you can write to carry out monotonous DOS-related tasks at your command. For example, if you frequently find yourself wanting to see a list of the files on drive B, sorted by file name, you can create a batch file that takes the drudgery out of manually typing the necessary commands and switches.

Or perhaps like me, you only use the DOS Shell from time to time and find yourself constantly typing DOSHELL or DOS SHELL instead of DOSSHELL. You can create a small batch file that runs the program whenever you type DS and press ↵.

Batch files are also handy when things need to be done in a certain (often obscure) order. For instance, computer folk often set up batch files to run network software, connect printers, etc. You can include virtually any DOS command or switch in a batch file.

Incidentally, each time you turn on your computer, it runs a special batch file called AUTOEXEC.BAT. It's a list of instructions your computer performs whenever you power up or restart your computer. To learn more about batch files—and there's plenty more to know—check out online help (type **HELP BATCH**) and the bigger books. Also, Lesson 18 will show you a way to see and change your AUTOEXEC.BAT file.

Creating Batch Files

Batch files are simple, unformatted "text files" containing legal DOS commands, names, paths, and other switches. Batch files must always be saved with the file extension BAT. You can create them with the MS-DOS Editor (type EDIT at the DOS prompt), with word processing programs that save "ASCII" files, or by simply typing commands from the keyboard using something called the COPY CON command. Let's try creating a batch file *that* way.

Suppose you wanted to create a batch file that lists the contents of a disk in drive B sorted by name. You already know how you would type the necessary commands manually, right? You'd type DIR B: /S /O | MORE and press ↵ each and every time you wanted to look at the contents of drive B.

Why so fancy you ask? Well, you never know when a disk is going to have subdirectories, so the /S switch is there just in case. The /O sorts the resulting list by file name (showing a list of subdirectories first). The | MORE pipe is included in case there are a lot of files to see.

Now that you know the command sequence you plan to use, let's try creating a batch file called DIRB.BAT:

1. Switch to the root directory, if necessary (type CD \ and press ↵).

2. Type COPY CON DIRB.BAT.

3. Press ↵.

4. Type DIR B:/S /O | MORE.

5. Press F6 (^Z will appear at the end of the line).

6. Press ↵. DOS should respond with the message "1 file(s) copied."

```
C:\>copy con dirb.bat
dir b: /s /o | more^Z
        1 file(s) copied

C:\>
```

That's it. You're done.

Note Pressing the F6 key in step 5 is just an obscure way of telling DOS you are done entering the commands for your batch file.

To test your first batch file:

1. Insert a floppy containing some files (and ideally multiple subdirectories).

2. Type DIRB and press ↵. A sorted list of files should appear. If there are more files than you have screen real estate, DOS will pause, waiting for that mysterious "any key."

3. Press the spacebar or nearly any other key.

Wanna try another? Here's the recipe for that quick way to run the Shell I mentioned earlier:

1. Switch to the root directory, if necessary (type CD \ and press ↵).

2. Type COPY CON DS.BAT and press ↵.

3. Type C:\DOS\DOSSHELL.

4. Press F6 (^Z will appear at the end of the line), and press ↵. DOS should respond with "1 file(s) copied."

To test this batch file, type **DS** and press ↵. Poof. The Shell should appear.

Is this cool, or what? You bought a Quick & Easy book this morning, and now you are a computer programmer. Well, almost. Don't quit your day job yet. Real programmers do most of their programming in "languages" containing hundreds of powerful tools. Batch programming uses nine special commands (Call, Choice, Echo, For, Goto, If, Pause, Rem, and Shift). Read about them online or in the big books.

Places to Put Your Batch Files

It's considered bad form to clutter your root directory with things like batch files (except the AUTOEXEC.BAT file, which must be in the root).

That's why I like to create a subdirectory called BATCH, or maybe BAT if I'm in a lazy mood. I put my batch files there and make sure that my new subdirectory is included in the PATH statement in my AUTOEXEC.BAT file.

Huh? Read on. The next lesson will clarify what the path is all about.

18

Changing Where DOS Looks with the PATH Statement

5 MINUTES

By now you've probably noticed that sometimes when you issue commands at the DOS prompt without typing the entire path, you get the message "File not found or bad file name." Other times, things work as expected. One reason for this is a line of instructions called the PATH statement in your AUTOEXEC.BAT file. It is a list of the disk drives and subdirectories that you want DOS to search when it can't find things in the "current" subdirectory.

For example, if you are "logged onto" the root directory and you type the name of a DOS command that is located elsewhere (in the DOS subdirectory, for instance), DOS begins by looking for the requested file in the root directory, then it starts looking in *only* the other subdirectories listed in your PATH statement.

If the DOS subdirectory is in your PATH statement (normally it is), eventually DOS will look there and find the file.

At first glance, it seems reasonable to conclude that you should simply include each subdirectory in your PATH statement and have DOS *always* look *everywhere,* right? Well, in a very simple system that might be practical, but usually it's not a good idea.

First, it's a pain to continually add subdirectories to the PATH statement each time you or some installation program creates a new subdirectory. Second, it takes time for DOS to search subdirectories, and, if you know there are places you don't want it to search, leaving those out of the list can speed things up. Finally (and perhaps most hideously), if you happen to have two different programs with the same name

(Quicken and Quattro, which are both named Q.EXE, for instance), this ambiguity can confuse DOS.

Here's how. When DOS searches your entire disk it will use the first match that it finds. It searches subdirectories in the order they appear in the PATH statement. So, you could be hoping for Quicken and get Quattro (or visa versa).

Do You Really Want to Do This?

Changing the DOS PATH statement is not for the faint of heart. While you can't do any permanent damage to your computer, you can render it temporarily brain-dead if you mess up your AUTOEXEC.BAT file. If you feel comfortable with some short-term aggravation, and if you have access to a computer person to help if things go wrong, feel free to actually try changing your PATH statement. Otherwise, just read this lesson to see how it is done, then ask for help and watch the first time.

Begin by making a copy of your working AUTOEXEC.BAT file on a floppy, just in case.

Backing Up Your Old AUTOEXEC.BAT File

1. Place a formatted, non–write-protected floppy in one of your disk drives (B: in this example).

2. While logged into the C:\ directory (the root), type

COPY AUTOEXEC.BAT B:

3. Press ↵. You should see confirmation of a successful copy:

```
C:\>copy autoexec.bat b:
       1 file(s) copied

C:\>
```

Using EDIT to Change the AUTOEXEC.BAT File

There are several ways to edit the AUTOEXEC.BAT file. Perhaps the easiest is to use the MS-DOS Editor—a small word-processing program that saves files as plain, unembellished "ASCII" text.

To edit the AUTOEXEC.BAT file (or any other text file), simply type the command EDIT, a space, and the complete name (and perhaps the path) of the file to be edited. For instance, at the C:\ prompt, you'd follow these steps:

1. Type EDIT AUTOEXEC.BAT.

```
C:\>edit autoexec.bat
```

2. Press ↵. You will see a window like the following one, displaying at least part of your AUTOEXEC.BAT file. Notice that there is an online help choice on the far right side of the menu bar. (Pressing F1 also brings up help.)

Quick Easy

The Help choice

```
   File   Edit   Search   Options                              Help
┌─────────────────────── AUTOEXEC.BAT ───────────────────────┐
│LH /L:0;1,42384 /S C:\DOS\SMARTDRV.EXE                        ↑
│echo off
│PROMPT $P$G
│PATH C:\DOS;C:\BAT;C:\UTIL;C:\PNTALK;C:\WINDOWS;C:\ADAM;C:\DOSAPS;C\:TIF;C:\WI
│
│SET TEMP=C:\TEMP
│SET SOUND=C:\ADAM\SBPRO
│SET BLASTER=A220 I7 D1
│
│REM LH /L:1,6400 C:\DOS\DOSKEY /INSERT
│LH /L:1,13984 C:\DOS\SHARE.EXE /L:200
│c:dosaps\snap\snap
│rem C:\DOS\DOSSHELL
│REM cls
│REM echo 1. Windows and Network
│REM echo 2. Treehouse
│REM echo 3. Windows no network
│REM echo 4. Parrot
│REM echo 5. Pro-Organ
│REM echo 6. Voice Editor II
│REM echo 7. Dr. Sbaitso                                       ↓
│←                                                           →│
 MS-DOS Editor   <F1=Help> Press ALT to activate menus          00004:019
```

The PATH statement

3. Examine the displayed text. One of the lines near the beginning of the file starts with the word PATH. Find it.

4. Use the arrow keys or the mouse to move the cursor to the
point where you want to edit the PATH statement. For instance, to change the subdirectory named BAT to BATCH,
move the cursor to the left of the semicolon after BAT and
type **CH**.

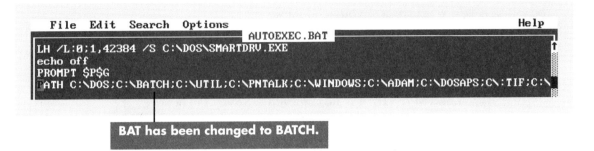

BAT has been changed to BATCH.

Sometimes, PATH statements are pretty long. To see text that is off the right edge of the screen, keep pressing → or use the mouse and the horizontal scroll bar at the bottom of the screen.

• Note Notice that path entries include all the necessary subdirectories (and optionally disk names) necessary for DOS to find the subdirectory. Each entry (except for the last one) is followed by a semicolon.

5. When you are finished editing the file (adding or deleting path names, for instance), choose Exit from the File menu.

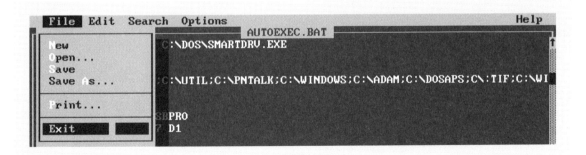

You'll be asked if you want to save your changes.

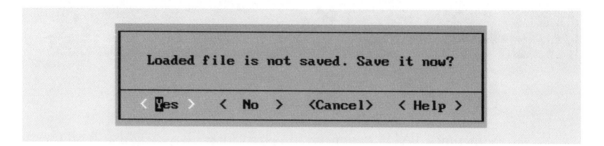

6. Choose **Yes** to replace the old file with the new one. Choose **No** to quit without saving the changes. Choose **Cancel** to go back to the Editor without saving to disk. Either use your mouse or move the little underline thingie with your **Tab** key, then press ↵ to make a choice.

That's it for editing the PATH statement (or any other item in a text file for that matter). You can also use another text editor instead of the MS-DOS Editor. Just be sure to save your work as a plain ASCII file, without any fancy formatting.

In the next lesson, you'll learn all about protecting your computer against viruses.

19

Protecting Your Computer from Virus Infections

For reasons that I will never understand, some wags write programs that spread silently from computer to computer, causing mischief as they creep. These virus or Trojan horse programs are spread when you put "infected" floppy disks in your computer or download infected files from dial-up bulletin board services via a modem. If your computer is connected to a network, you can also get them through that route.

Some of these programs just make your computer behave badly (beep strangely, work slowly, etc.). Some of the nastier programs actually destroy data and can cause you *major* headaches.

You can avoid these problems completely if you never put floppy disks in your computer, never dial up a bulletin board, and never connect to a network. But that's like spending your whole life standing in a doorway because there might be an earthquake. It's not very practical and it's sure no fun.

So the next best thing is to "take precautions," as Dad used to say. Here are some suggestions:

- Don't take files on floppies from strangers (at swap meets, user groups, etc.). If you have a home computer, warn your children about this problem. Kids are forever playing "pass the floppy."

- Don't exchange "stolen" copies of software. Buy the real thing from reliable dealers and manufacturers.

- Check your hard disk regularly with tools like Microsoft's Anti-Virus (it comes with DOS 6).

- Check floppies with tools like Microsoft Anti-Virus *before* you copy files from the floppies to your hard disk.

- Keep your detection software up-to-date. New viruses are created practically every week. There are even virus-detection software upgrade *subscription services* worth your consideration.

The easiest way to detect and eradicate the nasties is with the Windows version of Anti-Virus. It's installed automatically by DOS 6 if you have Windows on your machine. Let's take a look.

Using Anti-Virus for Windows

1. With Windows running, go to the Microsoft Tools window and double-click on the Anti-Virus icon:

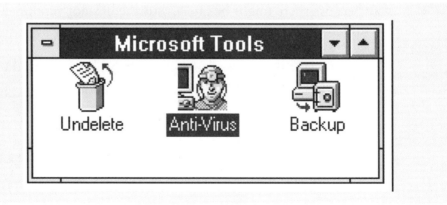

In a moment you'll see the Microsoft Anti-Virus window:

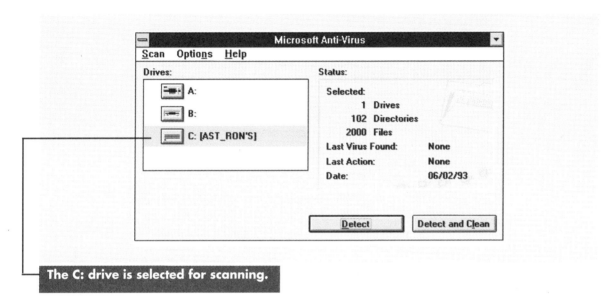

The C: drive is selected for scanning.

● Note Online help is available here. It's a good idea to check it out, if you haven't already.

2. Select the drive or drives you wish to inspect by clicking on the corresponding icons (**C:** in this example). You'll see a message as the directory is read. To select multiple drives, hold down the Shift key while you click.

3. Click on either the **Detect** or **Detect and Clean** button to start the scanning process. (The first time you run this program, choose **Detect**).

You will see a progress screen like this one as the program scans your disk or disks:

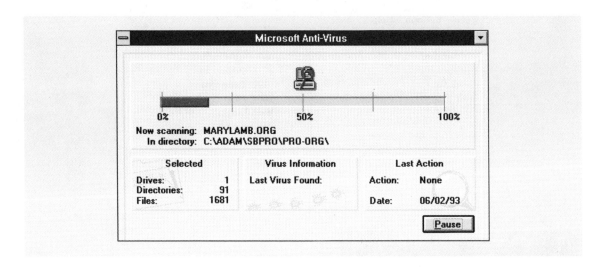

Eventually, you'll get either good news or bad news. Here's an example of good news—a status report:

If there is a virus, you will see it noted in this column.

	Scanned	Infected	Cleaned
Hard Disks	1	0	0
Floppy Disks	0	0	0
Total Disks	1	0	0
COM Files	41	0	0
EXE Files	219	0	0
Other Files	1737	0	0
Total Files	1997	0	0
Scan Time	00:01:44		

4. If all is well, you can click OK to quit Anti-Virus or check another disk.

5. To quit Anti-Virus, choose Exit from the Scan menu.

If Problem Files Are Detected

If the sweep finds one or more problem files, don't panic. Generally Microsoft Anti-Virus or another utility can rectify the situation. But if you are a newfie, this might be a good spot to stop and call the guru. That's why I suggested that you use the "detect only" choice for the first scan.

If the guru is unavailable, consider calling Microsoft Product Support to let them talk you through the options at this point. After all, they've seen a lot more of this than you have.

If there is no guru, and if Microsoft Product Support is gone for the night, and you need to continue using your computer before help arrives, rescan the disk using the Detect and Clean choice. Maybe you'll get lucky.

Using Anti-Virus for MS-DOS

There is a version of Anti-Virus that does not require Windows, called MSAV. It is not installed automatically and must be added with the Setup /E command described in your Microsoft manual. Once MSAV is installed, use its online help and the bigger books to learn more about it.

Preparing a Boot Disk Just in Case

Regardless of which version of Anti-Virus you use, it is an extremely good idea to create a floppy disk that you can use to start your computer in case

a virus messes up critical files in your root directory. Follow
these steps:

1. Place a non–write-protected floppy in the drive. This disk
   should not have any files that you need on it since the steps
   that follow will wipe them out.

2. If the disk is in your A: drive, at the DOS prompt, type
   FORMAT A:/S and press ↵. DOS will format the disk and
   put the necessary system files on it.

```
C:\>format a: /S
```

3. When formatting is finished, remove the disk, label it, and
   test it as follows: Place the disk in your floppy drive and
   warm-boot (restart) the computer by pressing Ctrl-Alt-
   Delete.

4. Once you are sure the boot disk works, remove it and warm-
   boot your computer again, to use the system files on your
   hard disk.

20 Maximizing Disk Space: DoubleSpace and Other Tricks

10 MINUTES

When you bought your computer, you thought the salesperson was trying to con you when she said an 80MB hard disk wouldn't be big enough in the long run, so you overruled her. Now you're out of disk space only six months later. Well, Bunky, you're not alone. You've just obeyed one of Mansfield's laws: "We always buy too little hardware too often."

There are things that you can do to get more available disk space— some fairly painless, others a potential trip to hell. Here are the typical alternatives (in my order of preference):

- Delete needless and duplicate files.

- Delete needless and duplicate files (just in case you missed alternative 1).

- Archive seldom-used files to floppies or tape.

- Clean up "lost" clusters.

- Purge (empty) your SENTRY subdirectory if you have one.

- Turn off Delete Sentry (use the Standard Protection or De-lete Tracker option instead).

- Buy a bigger hard disk (perhaps one with removable media).

- Use DoubleSpace or some other file squasher.

Deleting Unwanted Files

It seems almost too obvious, but it's a very common problem: People fail to throw out old, unneeded files on a regular basis. Mark your calendar. Every three months have a file-trashing party.

Some programs add to this problem by automatically making backup copies of each file that you create. If that's the case, and if you are sure you can live without two copies of the same thing on the same disk (this is not the same as a true off-site backup), turn off the automatic backup feature in your programs and delete the unwanted extra files that are already on your hard disk.

Your Microsoft manuals list some DOS files that you can remove if there are certain DOS 6 and/or Windows features that you never use. Since the list would fill a book this size, I won't repeat it here.

Archiving Seldom-Used Files

It's perfectly acceptable to move seldom-used files to floppy disks to free up disk space (this is called "archiving"). Then when you need a file, copy it back, or even work with it right on the floppy. Label these working archive disks carefully and store them in a convenient location. Just be sure you keep *additional* copies of these files off-site as true backups (see Lesson 11).

Cleaning Up "Lost" Clusters With CHKDSK /F

Occasionally, DOS will "lose track" of some available disk space. It sometimes does this when an application program crashes with files open. Over time, this can rob you of quite a bit of disk space. Here's what you can do to recover "lost cluster" space:

1. From the DOS prompt, type **CHKDSK /F** and press ↵.

• Note Always exit Windows before you do this. Windows must *not* be running.

DOS will list the number of lost clusters found (2895 in the example). It will ask if you want to convert the lost clusters ("chains") to files.

```
C:\>chkdsk /f

Volume AST_RON'S    created 01-08-1992 10:35a
Volume Serial Number is 1A8F-7A43

    2895 lost allocation units found in 7 chains.
Convert lost chains to files (Y/N)?
```

Potentially there is about 6MB of disk space that can be recovered (each allocation unit takes about 2K of space).

2. If you type **N** (the easy route), the space will be made available automatically. A more conservative approach is to type **Y**, which will cause lost clusters to be converted to files ending with the extension CHK.

Quick&Easy

```
Convert lost chains to files (Y/N)?y

120971264 bytes total disk space
    210944 bytes in 32 hidden files
    204800 bytes in 87 directories
 112764928 bytes in 1826 user files
   5928960 bytes in 7 recovered files
   1861632 bytes available on disk

      2048 bytes in each allocation unit
     59068 total allocation units on disk
       909 available allocation units on disk

    655360 total bytes memory
    359472 bytes free

C:\>
```

**The space is still being used. These recovered
files need to be moved or deleted.**

3. If you think these files may be of value (you've had a recent
crash in some important project), save the resulting files to
floppies or elsewhere. You can list them by typing DIR

```
FILE0000 CHK        2048 04-27-93  11:30a
FILE0001 CHK        2048 04-27-93  11:30a
FILE0002 CHK        2048 04-27-93  11:30a
FILE0003 CHK       18432 04-27-93  11:30a
FILE0004 CHK     5564416 04-27-93  11:30a
FILE0005 CHK      337920 04-27-93  11:30a
FILE0006 CHK        2048 04-27-93  11:30a
         7 file(s)      5928960 bytes
```

Here the files are in the root directory.

*.CHK at the DOS prompt.

4. Once you are certain that you don't need the information in

```
C:\>del *.chk
```

the lost clusters (with the help of a techie, perhaps), use the DOS ERASE or DEL command to remove the files and recover the space.

```
C:\>chkdsk

Volume AST_RON'S    created 01-08-1992 10:35a
Volume Serial Number is 1A8F-7A43

 120971264 bytes total disk space
    210944 bytes in 32 hidden files
    204800 bytes in 87 directories
 118749184 bytes in 1837 user files
   1806336 bytes available on disk
```

After deleting the .CHK files, there's still less than 2MB of free space. What's going on here?

5. Type **CHKDSK** a second time (no need for the /F switch here) to show the disk statistics indicating more free space (compare this illustration with the second one in the lesson):

But the space hasn't been freed, Mansfield. What gives?

Well, campers, it seems that if you have Delete Sentry turned on, disk space isn't really freed up when you delete things. All those .CHK files

are now in my SENTRY subdirectory (albeit with different names).
You need to purge your SENTRY subdirectory if you have one.

Purging Your SENTRY Subdirectory

If you have Delete Sentry enabled (see Lesson 10), files aren't actually
deleted for quite a while. They hide out in the SENTRY subdirectory,

**There! They were in the SENTRY subdirectory
with a bunch of other stuff.**

```
     Delete Sentry control file contains  210 deleted files.

Confirm purging of SENTRY files on drive C (Y/N).
y
```

but you can't just delete them from there using the DEL or ERASE

```
120971264 bytes total disk space
   155648 bytes in 5 hidden files
   196608 bytes in 86 directories
 95684608 bytes in 1657 user files
 24934400 bytes available on disk

     2048 bytes in each allocation unit
    59068 total allocation units on disk
    12175 available allocation units on disk

   655360 total bytes memory
   359472 bytes free
```

After purging there is nearly 25MB of free space.

command. If you are certain that you haven't recently deleted anything you'll want to recover in the near future, the following command at the DOS prompt will often free up tons of space: UNDELETE /PURGE. You'll be asked to confirm the purge:

There! now I have nearly 25MB of free space—for the moment at least.

Turning Off Delete Sentry

If you are short on space and long on confidence, you can turn off Delete Sentry altogether. Simply choose a different UNDELETE option (Standard or Delete Tracker), as described in Lesson 10.

Bigger Hard Disks

Purchasing a bigger hard disk is potentially the easiest but admittedly most expensive alternative.

- Decide how much space you think you'll need over the life-time of your computer, then double it.

- Make a complete backup of your current hard drive, and take your pride and joy to a reliable dealer.

- If there is room and an ample power supply in your computer, keep the old drive and add a new one (a D: drive, for example).

- Don't pay for the installation until you see everything running right.

> **● Note** You can add hard drives yourself, and you might save some money by ordering them through the mail—but this is no place for beginners. If you decide to take screwdriver in hand, be really, really sure you have good backups of your important stuff; and don't be surprised if it takes a while to get things working right. Be prepared to pay a dealer or consultant or repair person if you screw up. It'll probably cost more and take longer on your own if things don't go right.

DoubleSpace and Other File Compressors

I promised a skeptic's-eye view of DOS 6, and this is likely to get me in trouble, but here goes. There are programs that claim to double your disk space by storing "compressed" versions of your files on disk, then uncompressing them when needed. DOS 6 comes with a very good one called *DoubleSpace.* It may be the primary reason that you purchased DOS 6. It may already be at work on your computer. It is *not* installed on any of my computers and *never will be.* Here's why.

Disk doublers rarely double your available disk space, and you'll still need a portion of your disk that is "uncompressed."

All disk-related tasks take time. Compressing files before they are saved and then decompressing them when you need to use them often slows down your computer.

Computers are not 100 percent reliable, and occasionally they make mistakes. It stands to reason that the more steps you put between you and your data, the better the odds that something will go wrong. (Some at Microsoft disagree, arguing that since your disk drive is the least reliable part of your system, it is better to use less of it. By compressing, they claim, you are actually *less* likely to have a problem. But since you'll probably end up using your whole disk eventually anyway, I discount this theory—you'll be putting even more data at risk in the future.)

There are programs that are incompatible with disk compression schemes and some files that should *never* be compressed (including a few that Windows uses regularly). While DOS 6 takes care of most of that for you, who knows for sure if every oddball file you now have or may one day have will always be in the right place (the uncompressed part of your disk).

If you change your mind about DoubleSpace, it is a very tedious, time-consuming process to go back to the good old days. If you are like me, things go wrong when you are in a hurry. The last thing you'll want to do in a crunch is spend an hour or two or three on the phone while someone talks you through the steps of removing DoubleSpace and its effects from your disk!

Finally, DoubleSpace uses about 40K of conventional RAM (unless you and a techie move it out of conventional RAM). Conventional RAM is *always* in short supply—'round here, at least.

Using DoubleSpace on Your Hard Disk

If you or someone else followed the on-screen installation instructions for DoubleSpace when you installed DOS, DoubleSpace may already be running on your computer. Use the computer normally, and DOS will handle the details.

Since there's no easy way to shut off DoubleSpace, enjoy the extra room on your disk. It is very likely that you will be pleased with this feature.

Where Do I Go from Here?

In the short amount of time it's taken you to work through the lessons in this book, you've learned most of the things you'll ever need to know about DOS. Even the most advanced users of DOS spend most of their time doing the things you've learned from this book. Still, you might reach a point where you want to know a little more about DOS's other capabilities. After all, there are over a hundred commands you can amuse yourself with!

If you'd like to stick with a beginner's approach, learning in short, easy lessons and trying things out step-by-step, **The ABC's of DOS 6**, Alan Miller, SYBEX, 1993, is the right book for you. It covers the material in this book with a little more explanation, and then continues and explains some of the more useful advanced features.

If you think you're ready for a full-length reference work, check out Judd Robbins's **Mastering DOS 6 Special Edition**, SYBEX, 1993. It explains everything from the most basic topics to the most advanced.

If you'd like a quick-reference book to answer occasional questions, then you might want to check out another book I've written: **DOS 6 Quick & Easy Reference**, SYBEX, 1994. You can also try **DOS 6 Instant Reference**, Robert Thomas, SYBEX, 1993.

EASY DOS IT.

300 pp. ISBN:1234-X.

The *ABC's of DOS 6* is a straightforward beginner's guide to DOS 6 on a PC. This hands-on book gives you everything you need to make to make the most of DOS 6.

Even if you've never used a computer before, you'll get all the skills you need from *The ABC's of DOS 6*. In just a few lessons, you'll be completely comfortable with DOS 6.

Get up to speed on the latest powerful features of DOS. In no time, you'll be able to use the new DOS 6 utilities, including Double-Space, the utility that lets you double the storage capacity of your hard disk.

Sybex. Help Yourself.

2021 Challenger Drive
Alameda, CA 94501
800. 227.2346

SYBEX

A MONARCH'S MANUAL.

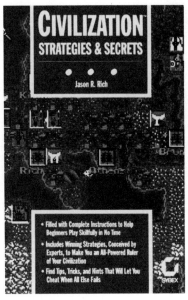

AN $800 SEMINAR
DISGUISED AS A BOOK

757 pp. ISBN:1259-5.

Get the same valuable information the many have paid over $800 to receive for less than $30. With *The Complete PC Upgrade & Maintenance Guide*, you'll be able to solve almost any PC problem and even supercharge your own machine.

You'll be able to use this book to install circuit boards and hard drives, increase the memory in your machine, add sound cards and other multimedia capabilities and avoid unnecessary expensive repairs.

Precise, step-by-step instructions make it easy for you to repair and upgrade your PC yourself. You'll get complete explanations of background and underlying concepts vital to PC maintenance. Armed with this information, you'll know always know what to fix, what to leave alone and when to call for help.

SYBEX. Help Yourself.

2021 Challenger Drive
Alameda, CA 94501
800-227-2346

SYBEX